PUF

Edito

MAGNOI

Val 'dashed up the fi
for a kick from the shadows
springs. At the moment he did not feel a debonair
gangster any more, but a frightened hungry boy who was up against heavy odds.'

This is part of what life is like in Magnolia Buildings where twelve-year-old Val lives with his Mum and Dad, two sisters, fourteen-year-old Ally, who longs for glamour, eleven-year-old Doreen, who longs for a scholarship, and his brother Len, who longs for a pet.

All the Berners live life to the hilt in their own way, but they haven't much money to do it on, and sometimes the shortage leads them into trouble and temptation, such as when Val 'finds' a purse, and Ally wrecks the school pantomime.

This is a splendid family tale. It is 'true' in the best sense, although not every family can have the good luck to have an Aunt Glad, with a lucky premium bond, as a lodger.

For readers of ten and over.

Cover design by Dick Hart

ELIZABETH STUCLEY

MAGNOLIA BUILDINGS

*

Illustrated by Dick Hart

PUFFIN BOOKS

in association with The Bodley Head

Puffin Books, Penguin Books Ltd, Harmondsworth, Middlesex, England
Penguin Books, 625 Madison Avenue, New York, New York 10022, U.S.A.
Penguin Books Australia Ltd, Ringwood, Victoria, Australia
Penguin Books Canada Ltd, 2801 John Street, Markham, Ontario, Canada L3R 1B4
Penguin Books (N.Z.) Ltd, 182–190 Wairau Road, Auckland 10, New Zealand

—

First published by The Bodley Head 1960
Published in Puffin Books 1965
Reprinted 1968, 1971, 1973, 1974, 1976, 1977, 1982

—

—

Set, printed and bound in Great Britain by
Cox & Wyman Ltd, Reading
Set in Intertype Plantin

CONTENTS

Chapter 1

ALLY'S NEW YEAR RESOLUTION

GLORIA BERNERS lay asleep in her bed at 49 Magnolia Buildings. She was fourteen years old and had been christened Gloria Evelyn, but the other children had always called her Glory Alleluia, and this had become Ally for short.

'New Year's Day!' said Ally to herself as she woke up. 'Got to wish for something.' She turned over on the pillow, and her mop of curly yellow hair made a fan round her face. She thought about the things she wanted. The first one was to get Doreen out of her bed for good. That would be grand. Doreen snorted in her sleep like a little pig.

She gave Doreen a good bump with her behind to stop her snoring.

Have a room to myself, that's next, she thought. Be glamorous like film stars. Meet Elvis Presley or Tommy Steele. Have some proper high heel shoes. Go to the Riviera for a holiday and wear a bikini.

That's too many wishes for one year, Ally said to herself. Fat lot of hope getting any of them. Not a chance of a room to myself, let alone a holiday on the Riviera.

No one had a room to themselves at 49 Magnolia Buildings. The buildings were a block of old-fashioned flats. Mum and Dad shared a room, the boys, Val and Len, who were twelve and eight, slept together, while Doreen, Ally, and Auntie Glad were in the third room. Not that Auntie Glad was much bother. She was so quiet and so small, almost a dwarf. When her mother had died, she had brought her own bed to Magnolia Buildings with her, and her trunk had just fitted under it. She took up very little cubic space at all. Nor did she speak at meals, but just slipped in and out to her dressmaking job, and no one ever noticed her.

But the boys took up all her share of space. Val was like twelve elephants. He never moved without carrying the entire landscape with him. Len played trains all over the floor. As for Doreen, there were her books on every table. She had to take her Eleven Plus exam this month. You would have thought she was the only girl in the world to take it, judging by the fuss she made. She's just cut out for a teacher, thought Ally.

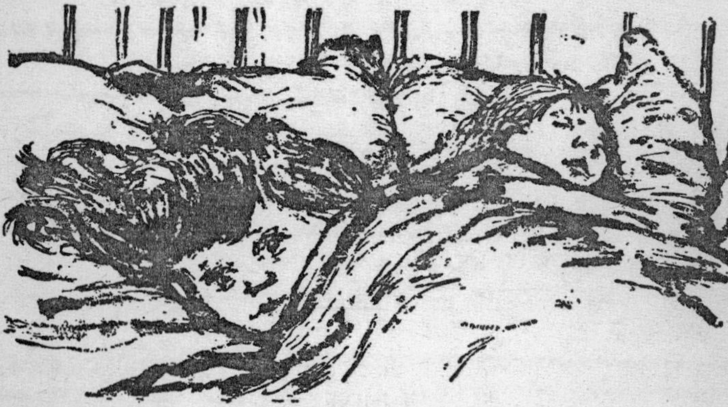

Then Ally remembered her diary. She must start to write it. Lou, her friend, had given her one for Christmas. Lou was going to keep a diary too, so that they could compare notes about all the exciting things that happened during the year. Ally lay and thought of the things she would write. This first day of the year was dark and snowing. Luckily it was a Saturday, and Dad was laid off for weekends as things were slack. Breakfast could be late.

Auntie Glad dressed under her nightgown in the dark and went off to wash in the scullery. The only water in the flat was there, and the bath was under the kitchen table.

Ally turned on the light and opened her diary. She wrote: 'Hullo New Year. Aren't you cold? We all live here in the flat. Mum, Dad, and Auntie Glad, Me, Val, Doreen, and Len. Auntie Glad came to live here when Dad's mum died. I wished for a lot of things this morning, but won't get them. I heard Mum go out to work at five. She is still cleaning offices but will be back for breakfast. Dad works on the railway. I must make the morning tea. . . .'

She went to put the kettle on when Auntie Glad came back to do her hair. They did not speak to each other. There was nothing to say at half past seven in the morning. It was too cold. Auntie Glad began taking out her curlers.

The kitchen smelt stuffy. Ally put on the hot water, then some cups and saucers on a tray and buttered a few slices of bread. Auntie Glad ate no breakfast, but she would be glad of a cup of tea.

Then Ally went to call the boys. They were both asleep in the one bed, with only Val's black curls and Len's crew cut showing above the sheet. Their clothes were flung on the floor, all mixed up with their dirty boots.

'Wake up,' shouted Ally. 'It's New Year's Day. And mind you wash.'

They did not stir. She shook Val. Glamour, she thought, what a hope! Picking up all the clothes off the floor, she threw them on top of the boys.

Val opened his eyes and shut them again. It was too cold to move. He could tell that by the tip of his nose. New Year's Day, he thought, perhaps this year I'll get my bike.

Dad was now shaving at the sink. It was like a jigsaw puzzle to fit in all the activities of the scullery. To an observer, the Berners family might seem to be performing a complicated dance as they washed, shaved, cleaned teeth and cooked meals. Ally laid breakfast for six while Auntie Glad slipped across the room and out of the door like a small grey mouse. No one saw her go. All she had done was to leave an empty cup with a few tea leaves in it.

Mum came back and the day really began. 'Cor, you ought to have been with us girls this morning,' she cried as she opened the door. 'Laugh! We nearly died. There was ice everywhere and the bus skidding about. We had that fat conductor. He's a

scream! Kept us all in fits. Mrs Beagle, she works in Shell, she gave as good as she got. Come on, let's have a cuppa. I'm dying for one.'

That was Mum all over, bringing the frosty morning and the jokes of the other cleaners home with her. She was always laughing and talking and always ready to sit down and have a cup of tea. Being stout these days, she was glad to take the weight off her feet. If the flat was usually rather untidy, well what of it?

'The house is made for the people, not the people for the house,' Mum would say, gathering up an armful of clothes and toys and shoving them into the nearest drawer. 'There's some as would rather have the room to that dirt that's brought in, but

I like a bit of company and a bit of fun. Come on, fill up and don't spare the sugar!'

There were always friends and neighbours sitting in Mum's flat. They came there to be cheered up and made to laugh. There's no marble halls about this place, thought Ally, but Mum makes it O.K.

'You got them trousers on again, Al?' asked Mum and she burst out laughing. 'Never saw such a lot as you girls are! We wore their faces in lockets, but you've got to have their names worked on your pants.' This was all because Ally had embroidered the names of Elvis Presley and Tommy Steele down the outsides of her blue jeans.

'All the others girls did it too,' she said, cross at being mocked. 'It's the fashion.'

'Stand on your heads, you lot would, if it was the fashion,' said Mum. 'Well, this won't keep baby. I must get a move on. You all going to the pictures this morning?'

On Saturday, the children all went to the cheap show at the cinema. It cost them only sixpence.

'I'm not going. I'm busy,' said Val.

Mum smiled and hoped he was not getting into mischief again. He was a good-looking boy with curly hair and dark eyes who was going to be tall. Val was usually in trouble.

'I'm going up to the pond to see if there's ice,' cried Len.

'Get out!' shouted Val. He always shouted, never talked. 'They won't let you on the ice. They break it up so us boys can't slide. Rotten, I call it. What's ice for?'

'They don't want you getting drowned,' said Dad. He was a big fair man with a droopy moustache. He never said much as it was impossible to out-talk Mum when she got started. Now he settled down to his pools. Doreen said she had to make a map of Europe.

'I don't want to go to the pictures, Mum.' Ally sounded sulky. 'It's kid stuff. Cowboys riding round that same old village. And who wants to see Mickey Mouse?'

'I do,' piped up Len. His pointed little nose was red with

the cold. 'Oh Mum, I do want to go. Or I'll miss the serial, *The Black Box*. It's ever so exciting. Last time, the monster man was in a dark cave and . . .'

'Go on, Ally, take him, do,' said Mum. 'I'm not having him crossing the High Street on his own.'

'Should think not,' said Dad.

'You go on now, Ally, and do the shopping, and then take Len.'

'It's a waste of money,' grumbled Ally. 'I want to go and see *A Heart for a Coronet* next Wednesday. Now, that'll be a smashing picture.'

'I'll pay for you to go, if you'll just take Len now,' wheedled Mum.

Dad said, 'That's right. Chucking your money away!'

'That's what I work for, isn't it?' cried Mum with spirit,

her black eyes sparkling. 'So as to have a bit of money I can chuck away, and you not able to throw it in my teeth.'

She liked spoiling the children and waiting on them. She had spoilt them all, especially Len. But none of the family could resist Len, with his dimples, his funny nose, and his mouse-coloured crew cut.

'Mum never goes to the pictures ever,' said Doreen in an accusing voice to Ally.

'Shut up,' shouted Ally. 'Give me the basket. What do you want, Mum?'

Ally usually liked shopping. She was friends with everyone in the shops, and they often gave her a scrap more meat or an extra apple. But this morning she felt sour. It was New Year's Day, and something wonderful ought to be happening. Something with a spot of glamour.

Outside, the air was sparkling and full of frost. It was an exhilarating day. Even old Sprot, the flats' caretaker, was whistling to himself as he shuffled about the yard. He hated all children and regarded them as natural nuisances. He would have liked to let the flats to no one but old age pensioners and spinster ladies.

Ally and Len ran across the Common. The tired old London trees were glistening, and there were icicles on the Temperance fountain. Alas, the park keepers must have got up very early to break the ice into lumps that looked like yellow candy. Small boys were already throwing the lumps at each other.

Yes, it was just the day for a foreign Count in an astrakhan collar to drive up and announce that Ally was really a foreign princess in disguise who had been dumped on the doorstep of 49 Magnolia Buildings as a baby, and that he was taking her off to reign over Ruritania where there had just been a revolution, and they were longing to welcome back their long lost queen. All Ally's ideas about the world beyond the Common she had gleaned from the pictures or TV because she had never been anywhere else.

'Oh come on, Len,' she scolded now, because all small boys

are awful to walk with. Either he went round and round under her feet like a puppy on a cord, or he lagged behind and got stuck at crossings.

There was a long queue outside the cinema. When the doors were opened, the children rushed in, shouting with excitement. Ally had bought some sweets to suck, in case it was a dull film. But after a while, she did get interested in the picture. There was one girl who really had glamour in spite of her old-fashioned clothes. Lucky thing! What a time she had! Held up in stage coaches, carried off on horseback, tied to railway tracks, dumped, gagged, in mines. And never a hair out of place, and a dress cut so low you'd think she must die of pneumonia.

'I've got to have glamour,' Ally said to herself. On the way to the pictures, she had caught sight of her own reflection in a shop window. Her pony tail of curls of which she was usually proud had looked – well, tatty. She had grown out of her coat, and her jeans seemed odd beneath it. She had a hole in her socks and her shoes were trodden crooked. They looked awful because she had not stopped to polish them that morning.

When the lights went up at the end of the film, she glanced at her hands. The nails were none too clean, one was broken and the cuticles were overgrown.

You need a bathroom to look smart, she said to herself. Nothing gets the dirt off like a proper long soak.

As the heroine was clasped to the hero's breast at last, Ally made her New Year's resolution. She was going to attain glamour, even if it killed her.

Chapter 2

THE BLACK HAND GANG

VAL went down the stone staircase of the block that Saturday morning. His coat collar was turned up, his hands were in his pockets that might or might not contain a gun. He walked with the special slouching swagger adopted by all gangsters. He also walked with precaution, because at any moment one of Shorty's gang might leap out and attack him. His life was as dangerous as a Chicago gunman's. It was one long battle in self-defence.

When he got to the yard, Sprot was shouting at some small children, a few mothers were passing with shopping baskets, or were shouting conversations up and down the balconies. Two of Val's own chaps were in sight, leaning up against walls and pretending to be part of the scenery. Val gave a very slight inclination of the head, and walked firmly across the centre of the yard. It was safer to keep clear of the walls, something might always drop from the balconies. The other chaps, pretending not to see him, presently walked out of the yard too, as though they had just remembered something important.

The three boys, George, Ginger, and Val, met on the Common. This was pretty safe, being near to the main road. 'Where's the others?' asked Val between closed teeth and looking in the opposite direction.

'Meeting us at the bandstand,' answered George in an equally muted voice.

'We'll go up separately,' hissed Val. 'Don't want to be seen in a bunch. Might arouse suspicion. See you later, alligator.'

He trotted briskly across the grass of the Common, dodging in and out of football games. The grass felt like wood shavings beneath his feet, for it was still frozen stiff. The other boys made separate detours through the trees, all the time keeping an eye on Val in case he should be attacked.

Something's got to be done about Shorty and his lot, Val was thinking as he panted along, blowing out little clouds of steam. They're a nuisance round the block. Time someone broke them up. It'll have to be me. None of the other chaps have got organization. That's what it wants, organization.

Shorty and his lot were a real menace. They were big boys, some of them fifteen or sixteen. They hadn't enough money to amuse themselves, and they weren't yet going steady with girls. So they just mucked about and beat up the younger boys. Val had been collecting his gang together all the winter. He was not by nature a gangster; in fact he would have been quite content with a peaceful life, but he was a natural leader. He wasn't going to have the small chaps beaten up and their bikes pinched or broken. Whatever people said about Val Berners, they always agreed he had a kind heart.

The bandstand was a good meeting place. It was fairly safe, being close to the café, where there were always plenty of people. If the worst came to the worst and Shorty and Co. turned up, they could dodge into the café. Shorty couldn't start anything in there.

Val wove his way through mothers and prams. Six of his chaps had turned up, but only four would be much good in a proper fight. There was George, a tall boy, but not as strong as he looked. He had broken two front teeth falling off his bike when Nap, Shorty's lieutenant, had put a stick in the front wheel. George had certainly got it in for Shorty's gang. George was a good chap and Val could trust him all right. Then there was Billy with the round, red face and stout little body. He was all right too, but a bit of a big mouth. You never knew when he'd split under questioning. Bert and Ginger were brothers. Bert was all right, but Ginger was a bit young, although he could run very fast. Brian was fifteen and by rights he should have been in Shorty's lot; but he was a quiet boy and scared of a rough crowd. He had joined up with Val for protection. Val didn't think a lot of him. He was not much of a fighter and spent most of his time reading in the public library. Eddy made up the six. He was such a thin child that Mum said he could go through a keyhole without turning the lock.

The boys faced Val with their backs to the bandstand. It rose above them on thin pillars that held up a pagoda-shaped roof. In the summer there were concerts on the platform. A locked door led to a sort of cellar below the stand.

'I know how to get in that old house,' said Val. 'But we've got to be careful, see, or we'll have the police on our tails again. You all know where it is? Bill, you got the candles?'

Bill produced a couple of candle ends out of his pocket.

'How did you get them?'

'Mum threw them out, Val.'

'Never told her anything?'

'No.'

'That's right then. Let's go.' They all went running across the grass. Now they were free of the yard, they could look like boys playing and not walk about being gunmen. When they got to the deserted house they deployed their forces. The house stood right in the middle of the Common. Fir trees grew close up to its dark, dirty windows that were broken by stones.

'Come in one by one and don't make a row,' said Val.

He slid behind some dark evergreen bushes that were powdered with frost. He was as good a stalker as any backwoodsman, for he spent his life evading enemies or justice. He was also an excellent climber because he spent the summer evenings like a marauding monkey, scaling all the garden walls for miles around, running along their broken glass tops, searching for fruit or flowers. Most of the fruit was not ripe, and he didn't really want the flowers, but it was the fun of the thing. No explorer can make a perilous voyage and come back without some treasure.

Now George unearthed a crowbar that he had hidden beneath some rubbish. He and Val inserted it into the lintel of the back door; but at that moment there came a low whistle from Ginger. All the boys fell into the bushes and froze. Presently, Ginger managed to crawl as far as Val.

'Bluebottles! Cops!' he whispered. 'Saw them on the road, two of them.'

After a while the policemen moved on and the boys went back to forcing the door. It gave suddenly with a loud report and the boys fell into the hall. They stopped a moment to listen and then Val said, 'Give us a light. It's dark as pitch in here.'

George struck a match and the boys surged forward.

'Get back!' Val gave a sidelong kick. Discipline must be maintained. 'And don't make a blooming row, or I'll learn you. Brian, pull the door to. Ginger, you stick about in the bushes.'

The house had that damp, sooty, smell of shut-up London houses. It was quite a big place but in a state of decay. The boys surged and jostled into the kitchen, almost taking the skins off their elbows in their excitement. The stove was rusty. The only thing on the fixed dresser were empty jam jars, and there were mice droppings everywhere.

'This'll do fine for headquarters,' said Bill, wagging his round head.

'Want to be copped, you ass?' asked Val calmly. 'No! Underground's the only safe place. The cellar!'

They had a look at the cellar. Coal must have been kept there, for it was black and the floor was gritty. 'This'll do fine.' Val held the candle high. With his handsome, dark head, he looked a real leader. Billy with his red face, and George with his gaping teeth could not compete with Val.

There was no need to explain to the chaps the uses of a safe, secret place. Every gang must have a hideout, somewhere to keep things and to cook food.

'Better have a look round upstairs. You never know,' said Val. 'Remember that picture when Cary Grant took over the empty house and never looked upstairs?'

'Yeah,' said George. 'But there was only a girl there.'

'Not *that* film.' Val was scornful. 'I mean the one with the time bomb inside the clock. He didn't half cop it.'

There was nothing on the top floor, not a dead body, a time bomb, nor even a girl. They did, however, find a rickety table in a dusty shuttered bedroom and carried it down to the cellar.

George looked at it with pride as he set it middlemost on the filthy floor. 'It's getting quite furnished,' he said.

'My mum's got an old methylated stove she never uses,' said Brian. 'I'll bring that next time and we could cook potatoes.'

Ginger who was supposed to be on guard, but had followed with the rest, now clapped his hand over Brian's mouth. 'Sh!'

There was certainly someone outside the house. They heard steps in the porch. 'Down the stairs all of you, and shut the cellar door, Ginger,' whispered Val. It might be the police, or, worse still, some of Shorty's lot. The boys all stood there, the candle blown out, their feet scrunching a little in the coal dust. Val was uneasy, for it would be awful if the cops caught them. He dare not get pinched again. He had had too many warnings already, and this would count as breaking and entering. Val knew as much about the law as any lawyer. If the police opened the cellar door, the boys would be caught like rats. And what would Mum say if Val were sent away to an approved school? Yet it wasn't possible in London to lead a law-abiding life and have some fun. Val could not exist without adventure.

There came a sound of heavy footsteps in the passage. The

policemen must have come back and noticed the forced door. That idiot Ginger could not have shut it properly.

'They've been in here again,' said a man's deep voice. 'I'll give them something when I catch up with them.'

'I thought I saw some of the little devils mucking about in the bushes,' said a younger, lighter voice.

'It's always Saturdays,' said the older man. 'They ought to go to school all day and every day of the week. Then we'd get a little peace.'

The boys gasped with horror in the darkness. Suppose the police got a new law made that said everyone was to stay at school the whole week long? That would be awful!

If the police did open the cellar door! In the darkness, all the boys could hear their hearts thudding. If this had been at the pictures, the Gestapo would have wrenched open the door and seen their pale faces, and then there would have been the spit, spit, spit, of machine guns, and they would have pitched over, seven lifeless corpses.

Heavy feet came past the cellar door and halted. The boys held their breath. Suppose someone hiccoughed now?

The deep voice remarked, 'I can't waste time here. You'd better report that door, Evans. You see about it.'

The heavy feet passed the cellar door again, and went down the passage, and the boys could hear the men fiddling with the broken door.

Ginger and George started to shove to get out. Val elbowed them back. 'Use your loaf,' he whispered scornfully. 'This is maybe a trick. No one is to move till I say so, see?' He jabbed his elbow backwards in the darkness and got Ginger in the stomach.

'Ow! You hurt me, Val.'

'Shut up. Or I'll cut your throat. I won't have you in the gang, see?'

The gang all stayed silent for a moment, thinking Val was wonderful. Anybody else would have gone rushing out and got caught. You had to use your loaf, just as Val said. No wonder he was the leader of the Black Hand Gang! That was their name, and a good one too, as their hands were always filthy and left traces on everything they touched.

'We'll give them five minutes,' said Val. 'Police haven't got patience. Then I'll make a reccy. You chaps stay here. If I don't come back, you'll know they got me. And keep your big mouths shut. We don't want to bust the whole place open.'

Val edged silently into the passage, shoved back Ginger's face with his filthy paw, and shut the cellar door. The police had propped up the broken door. Val crept towards it and put his eye to the keyhole. Through it, he saw a small area of holly bush and sooty grass. Then softly, inch by inch, he shifted the door and leapt back into shelter, waiting a moment for the attack, prepared to duck between invading legs. But no one moved. With a beating heart, he dared to step into the garden. Not a sound! The coppers had gone!

The getaway was as cautious as the arrival. Under Val's command, the boys left the house one by one and emerged as though facing a burst of machine-gun fire, dived into the bushes and crawled through a hole that someone had already made in the fence. Val and George replaced the door and made it look natural.

'You're a bit black,' said George to Val as they trotted back across the Common. Val looked as if he had spent a day down a coal mine.

'That's all right,' said Val comfortably. 'Mum's used to it.'

Chapter 3

RUBY

It was the Monday of the next week that Len brought home Ruby. He was always bringing home something, sparrows with broken legs, or stray kittens.

Mum had been washing all day, and had just brought up the first lot of dry things as the children came out of school. Len walked slowly upstairs, leading Ruby by the hand.

She was a small, fat girl from Jamaica, very black, with woolly hair that was tied into bunches with red bows. All the way up the stone stairs she sobbed loudly. Her nose was running and her knees were scratched and bleeding. Len kept talking to her in a soothing voice. 'Come along up then, Ruby. Mum'll make it all right.' She was still howling as he led her along the balcony and banged on the door of 49.

'What on earth?' began Mum, as she opened the door. 'Now, Len, I can't have any clutter here today. I've just brought in the wash.' Ruby howled louder.

'They've been mucking her about at school,' said Len, his own mouth trembling at the thought of the other children's cruelty. 'So I brought her home, see. It's not fair, Mum. It's not her fault she's black.'

'Oh, oh,' yelled Ruby.

Mum, who was really every bit as soft-hearted as Len wiped Ruby's nose with her apron, and picking up the sobbing little girl, carried her into the flat, with Len following behind like a worried sheep-dog who has found a sick lamb.

'There, lovey,' said Mum, sitting down with the child on her lap. 'What a shame then. Look at her knees! Len, pass me the cloth, no, the damp one, silly.' With a practised hand, she polished up the small black face with its flat nose, and then popped a toffee into the little, drooping mouth. 'What's your name, duck? Ruby? Well, isn't that a pretty name! And what a smart check frock you've got and lace on your petticoat! Why, aren't you the smartest girl in London?'

Len leant against Mum's chair. He was glad that Mum had stopped Ruby howling, for he couldn't bear tears; but he wasn't sure he liked to see her on Mum's lap. That was his place.

Ruby stayed to tea, and Len was sent over to her mother's to say where the child was. She was a nice little girl and soon cheered up over her chips and doughnuts.

'I got a bike,' she lisped.

'It's a blooming shame,' said Mum. 'I'll speak to the teacher.'

'The blacks oughtn't to come over here taking up our house room,' said Dad. 'Why, they're paying double rents to get flats, and our people without a roof over their heads. Why can't they stop in their own country?'

'Still, that's not Ruby's fault,' said Mum. 'Go on, duck, have another doughnut. Live and let live, I say. Why, Alf Berners, you might have been born with a black skin . . .'

'I wouldn't then,' said Dad with spirit. 'Both my parents being white. They were saying round the Cock the other night that our young people can't get married because there's nowhere for them to live.'

'Oh, they say a lot round at the Cock!' cried Mum, tossing her head. 'Come on, lovey, eat your cake and Dad'll take you home.'

Auntie Glad looked a little surprised when she came in to tea to see the small black visitor, but she said nothing, because she always kept herself to herself. She just went and fetched her own special cup and saucer painted with roses. She would not have mentioned it if Alf's wife had asked a crocodile to tea. After all, it was Alf's house.

So Dad took Ruby home and gave her a threepenny bit as well; but he only knocked at the door of Ruby's flat and hurried away, because he did not want to explain that the white children had been so cruel.

Mum said to Ally, 'I ought to speak to the teacher.'

'It won't be any good,' said Ally, 'the children don't do it when the teacher's there.'

Later in the evening, Mum remarked to Mrs Crawley: 'You never know what Len'll bring back next. He ought to be a missionary.'

Chapter 4

'I'VE JUST GOT TO TAKE IT'

THE next excitement was the Eleven Plus exam. Doreen really worked herself up into a state about it. She didn't say much, but her eyes grew pink from over-reading and she came out in spots. Mum dosed her but it made no difference.

'I wish they'd do away with this old Eleven Plus,' said Mum. 'Don't you bother with it, Doreen. If you pass, it only means a lot more homework and your Dad having to keep you when you ought to be earning a living.'

'Don't you want me to get on, Mum?' asked Doreen fiercely.

'Not if it brings you out in spots,' said Mum. 'And us not being able to turn on the TV because you can't concentrate. I'll run you round to the doctor tomorrow, to get you a tonic.'

'I can't go to the doctor and waste a whole morning's school,' cried Doreen.

Mum sighed and gave up. 'Well I'm sure I don't know,' she said.

But the night before the Eleven Plus exam, Ally was woken by Doreen being sick all over the floor. Disaster of this magnitude sent Ally to wake Mum, who was snatching those last precious moments before she had to scramble up and start to work.

Mum was used to night alarms, and at once clambered out on her tired legs, grabbed at her old coat, sent Ally for bucket and mop and to put on a kettle. With her head a mass of steel curlers, and her eyes still swollen with sleep, she went swiftly into the girls' room and bundled the shivery Doreen back to bed. 'There, ducky. Mum's here. Don't you cry.'

The child, her teeth chattering, lay down, while Mum piled the clothes on her, and then plied the mop with a practised hand.

'Cor, you have got yourself into a fine panjandrum over this exam.' Mum glanced at Doreen's face, green between the red, rat-tail hair on the pillow. 'I've a good mind to keep you in bed tomorrow.' She squeezed out the mop.

'No, no.' Doreen started up, and then sank back dizzily. 'I've got to get through the Eleven Plus. I've just got to take it, Mum. I'll never be a teacher if I don't.'

'There's other things you can be,' said Mum consolingly. But she knew in her heart that Doreen was destined to be a teacher, for ever since she could walk she had been playing at schools. She had sat her dolls in a row and taught them, she had taught Grandma's kitten, and even Len too, when he came along. Her favourite toy had always been a blackboard.

'Teach, teach,' cried Mum. 'Can't think where you get it from. Well there, you never know with kids. There's Glory Ally with her head full of nonsense about crooners and glamour, and Val heading straight for gaol for all I can see. Cor, what a family I've got! Not to mention what Len brings home.'

Doreen's face had grown yet more pale. She sat up clutching at the air. 'I'm going to be . . .' she gasped, and Mum had just time to shove the bucket before her.

When Doreen lay back spent and empty, Ally brought in the hot bottle and was sent to empty the bucket as Mum must get dressed and go to work. Doreen lay with shut eyes, thankful for the warmth, and prayed fervently. 'Please God, let me be well tomorrow, I mean today. I've just got to be a teacher. Please stop me being sick. Amen.'

Somehow, Doreen managed to get dressed by eight o'clock. Auntie Glad took no part in the discussion at breakfast about whether Doreen should go to school, just as she had never stirred during the alarums of the night. Perhaps she had decided that to pretend invisibility was the only way to live in her brother's house. She seldom spoke at meals, and the only time she talked was late at night to Mum. Then Ally, lying in bed, sometimes heard her speaking almost entirely in capital letters, as though the little dressmaker's secret nature would not let her use complete words. 'So I said to Miss G. it's t.t. for now, and if you think Miss S. doesn't k. you're very much m. about it.' Ally used to wonder what these mysterious stories were about, but guessed they must be the feuds amongst the workers in the dressmaking shop.

Meanwhile, Doreen was eating no breakfast, and scarcely swallowing her tea.

'You ought to be in bed, my girl,' said Dad gruffly through his drooping moustache. He hated the children to be ill. 'Girls don't need to pass exams. I never passed nothing in my life, and I get on all right, don't I?'

'Oh, let her go,' said Mum with the tolerance of experience. 'If she's sick, she's sick, and can come home again. But she'd better have a try or we'll never hear the end of it. I'll go with her and tell the teacher she's been poorly.'

Mum muffled Doreen up in a large scarf and led her out into the cold morning. Sea-gulls were paddling about in the drained pool, and there were dogs smelling the rimed grass. The sun had come up in a shrouded red ball.

'You going to get there?' asked Mum.

Doreen nodded bravely. There were blue shadows under her eyes, and her nose was peaked and sharp over the red folds of her scarf.

'If you feel sick, throw up and get it over, see?' said Mum.

Doreen nodded again. She dared not speak. All she could think of was that she must get to her desk and sit there. If she could do part of the exam, she told herself, they would have to let her finish it another day. To stop being sick, she kept thinking of the black children that she had seen in a missionary film. She had made up her mind that she was going to Africa to teach them. This plain, stolid little girl was just as much an adventurer as Val or Ally, and she had more determination than either of them.

As Mum and Doreen reached the chemist, the church clock struck nine. School did not start till a quarter past. Mum stopped dead, her eyes on the shop. 'They must have got something in there to stop sickness,' she said. 'A pink pick-me-up. That's it! I've heard of such things. Come on in, Doreen, and we'll get your stomach fixed.'

'No, Mum!' wailed Doreen, sticking in her heels like a little mule. 'It'll make me worse again.'

'Don't act so silly,' cried Mum, tugging her along. 'Do you want to be a teacher or not? Then just you do what Mum says.'

Doreen was marched up the steps into the old-fashioned shop. And then Mum said to Mr Jimson behind the counter, 'I want one of those pink pick-me-ups.'

Mr Jimson grinned. 'Been on the tiles again, Mrs Berners?' He knew Mum well, for she was always in and out to fetch her tonic or some corn plasters.

'Get on with you!' Mum began to laugh. 'No, it's for Doreen, here. She's got her Eleven Plus today, and she's sick in her stomach. Now hurry up, ducks. We've got a quarter of an hour to get her right.'

'Rightyoh,' exclaimed Mr Jimson. 'I'll give the young lady a cocktail that would fix an earthquake. Won't be a minute.' And he dived out of sight.

'You sit down, Dor,' said Mum, lowering herself into a chair and sticking her swollen ankles and calves out before her. 'Just as cheap to sit.'

Doreen sat, looking at the immaculate green lino, and wondering what would happen if she threw up on that. Already the preliminary sweat and chill were starting again.

'Now,' said the chemist's voice. 'You drink this down. It'll soon put you right.'

Doreen took the glass with a shaking hand, and sipped and choked and spluttered. 'I – I can't,' she gasped. The stuff burnt her throat, and it had a strong, peculiar taste.

'Drink it up,' commanded Mum, her face red with anxiety. 'We've only got five minutes left.'

Doreen shut her eyes and drank. It was like living flame surging through her gullet, but she was of martyr stuff. She had to pass. She had to be a teacher. She would drink anything to succeed.

She did not remember much about the walk to the school, nor of Mum's explanations to the teacher. The mixture, whatever it contained, pushed the whole world a long way off, so that her feet seemed to tap a pavement that was miles from her brain. The awful chill and sweat had been replaced by a queer glow, as if the mixture had started a small fire inside her stomach. By the time she got to her desk and was given her paper, she felt suddenly light and cheerful, almost carefree. Doreen was a natural fusser who took life hard. But the pink mixture, working on an empty stomach, had taken away all the worry and left her able to sing or dance or to fly up in the air.

The first paper was the essay. There were four subjects from which to choose, but Doreen did not hesitate. She recognized her theme at once.

'What I want to be when I am grown up,' she wrote at the top of her page. 'If I cannot be a teacher and a missionary, and go to teach the black children of Africa, I shall die of grief . . .' She wrote and wrote in her clear neat hand, all the things that she had never told anybody, all the deep wishes of her heart. She described the joy she would find in teaching, and her burning desire to make other people love learning. The pink mixture had given her a strange, wonderful freedom, so that the words just poured off the end of her J nib, and formed sentences that were queer stuff to be written by an eleven-year-old girl.

The pink mixture carried her through the arithmetic as well, but it was beginning to lose its magic power by the time she reached the intelligence test. Her stomach felt empty now and her head was beginning to swim. But her determination held. She bent her will to solving such problems as: 'If James is the brother of Henry and Henry has six children, what relations are those children to James's father?' She examined squares and dots and all sorts of other squiggles, and worked out their sequences and relations. Her neat, precise mind took over when the inspiration of the pink mixture fell away.

And then, so odd is the working of the nervous system, the moment the examination was over, she felt quite well and went home to eat an enormous dinner.

'How did you get on?' asked all the family.

'All right,' said Doreen. 'Pass the bread, Val.'

'There, what did I say?' Mum asked triumphantly of Dad. 'Only nerves, see?'

'This here education of women's a lot of nonsense,' said Dad. 'The chaps at the Cock were saying so only the other week.'

'Frightened of their wives knowing a bit too much,' said Mum, laughing.

But Doreen was not listening. She had suddenly begun to blush. A terrible, hot shame filled her, for now she was beginning to remember what she had written in the essay, all her private thoughts and longings. What would the examiners, those cold, critical people, think of her? They must think she was a silly idiot! How awful! They would laugh at her essay for nonsense, and she would be sure to fail.

Mum looked across at her daughter. 'Well, you won't have to do any more work now, Dor. That's one good thing. You'll be able to sit and watch the TV and no nonsense.'

Chapter 5

GLAMOUR

ALL through February, Ally was trying to achieve glamour. She bought a bottle of nail varnish and she manicured her nails. The only trouble was that with so much washing up, the varnish did not stay on very well. She had to keep touching up the nails that had flaked and peeled, and the dirt got in between the coats of varnish and looked peculiar. She did not have enough money to buy any varnish remover.

'Looks like blood on your nails,' said Dad with distaste. 'You might have been gutting a rabbit.'

But Ally persisted. She went to bed at night in a row of pins and grips that were to preserve the set in her naturally curly hair; but while she slept, the pins fell out, and Doreen complained it was like sharing a bed with a hedgehog. Ally also spent a long time ripping out Elvis Presley's name from her pants and embroidering 'Izzy Waters'. It had been a long job, but was worth it to anyone who had heard Izzy crooning 'I love you Mondays, Tuesdays, Wednesdays, Thursdays', which was his latest hit tune.

Ally's best friend was Lou. They always walked to school together, giggling the whole way. They giggled because everything they said to each other sounded so funny. They also giggled because they were happy.

Mum had got Ally into the Senior Church School, because she had heard that the classes were smaller and that the head mistress tried to train the children in good manners. Ally liked school well enough, especially now she was in the top class and working with Miss Fleetwood.

Miss Fleetwood was different to the other, older teachers. She was very pretty and had been to Oxford as well as to the teachers' training college. Her father was a parson in the country.

'I think she's smashing,' said Ally to Lou as the two girls reached the High Street one spring morning.

'She talks a bit posh,' said Lou, 'but when she reads poetry, I get shivers down the back. It's so lovely. Gosh, and the way she looks at you, if you whisper or move.'

'She's got style, see?' said Ally. 'Not like the other teachers.'

'I can't stick Mr Grainger. The way he thinks he's funny,' agreed Lou. Lou was a brunette, and she greased and plastered down neat kiss curls all around her face so that her hair looked as if it had been painted on like a Dutch doll's. Out of school she usually wore tartan trousers and a blue duffle coat, dazzle socks and ballet shoes.

'Please, Miss Fleetwood, would you read the *Lady of Shalott*?' Ally asked in English that morning. The class was thrilled and sat listening to the teacher's clear young voice. There was something about the mysterious Lady that pleased them.

'Cor, miss,' said Ally at the end. 'They ought to do that on the TV I mean it'd make a smashing scene when she comes out and gets in the boat and lies singing till she dies and all the knights look at her and – and everything.'

'I wonder how Tennyson would have liked being on television?' asked Miss Fleetwood, smiling. 'Perhaps Byron would have liked it better. He loved publicity. Just listen to this now.' And she read them Byron's poem, *She Walks in Beauty Like the Night*. Ally got so worked up by this poem that she walked in beauty all that week, until Mum passed her crossing the Common, and asked, 'Got a crick in your neck?'

'Glamour!' thought Ally. 'What a hope!'

Ally had never quite worked out for herself where Glamour began and ended. To her it meant everything that was exciting and lovely. She was sure that it applied to Izzy Waters, because his strumming and singing stirred something inside her. She knew that certain actresses were glamorous, and so were certain clothes and scents and places. But now she was beginning to guess there was a rarer, more complicated glamour, something the poets had, and that Miss Fleetwood knew about. That was the fascination of Miss Fleetwood, and that was why Ally haunted her. She wanted to find out the secret thing that Miss Fleetwood knew.

The young teacher had not got the obvious glamour of Diana Dors. She was not dripping in mink and pearls, but she wore crisp, clean shirts, her hair was coiled up neatly on the nape of her slim neck, and there were little pearl studs in her ears. She smelt fresh too, of some sort of clean soap, not strong scent. Ally did not have a very complete picture in her mind of what a real lady should be, but she thought Miss Fleetwood might be it.

There was no fuss or scolding in Miss Fleetwood's classes. As she entered the room, everything became calm, pleasant and orderly. All the girls felt they were in for a treat. The young teacher moved gracefully and wrote on the blackboard in an elegant script. Even her books had plastic covers. Her shoes were very small and pretty. The girls would stop her in the corridor and ask, 'Are you teaching us today? Oh good!'

'When she comes into class,' Ally said to Lou, 'it's like as if someone had brought in a bowl of flowers.'

Lou giggled. 'That's right. And when old Tody comes in, it's as if someone had brought in a cut onion.'

Ally began to imitate Miss Fleetwood's clothes. She tried to smooth out the wild pony tail and to coil it neatly. All Mum said was, 'Skinned rabbit the fashion now?'

Ally also tried to wear crisp little blouses. She found a white one that Auntie Glad had brought home, but on Ally it didn't stay crisp. It got ink spots and sooty, and soon looked bedraggled. The shirt made a lot of washing and ironing.

Ally did not give up her allegiance to Miss Fleetwood, even though the next week she went to see Berta Mathews in *Love Lights*, and Berta was wearing a skin tight black sweater, huge gold earrings, and a gipsy head-scarf. Ally took in the side seams of her old navy jersey, borrowed a couple of Mum's curtain rings, and Dad's red cotton hanky. Then Val said, 'You sella di ice creama, no?'

'It's no good trying in this family,' cried Ally bitterly. 'I'm young, I've got to experiment to find my type.'

On Thursdays, the Rector or the Curate came to take a short service at the school. None of the girls liked the Curate because he was wet and tried to be hearty, but they liked the Rector. He was a shy, absent-minded man who should have been a don at a university. He always looked tired from over-work, but he talked to the girls about whatever happened to be in his mind, using the same words as he would have spoken to a gathering of bishops. To him, one human being was as important as another, and he gave the smallest child all his attention.

Ally had never seriously thought about religion. Sometimes, she wondered if it were another sort of glamour, one of those strange, secret, unknown glamours that Miss Fleetwood knew about. There was not anyone with whom she could discuss this idea, because Lou would only have giggled. Anyhow she had not the words to express her vague feelings. Ally knew that having a boy and getting married was glamorous. Love was glamorous, the crooners said so. But it seemed rude to God, almost blasphemous, to put Him and religion into the same category. And yet somehow Ally felt that all these things were connected.

At home, Dad never went to church, and Mum always needed her lie-in on Sunday morning after getting up at five every other day of the week. Sometimes she took Ally along to evensong, because Mum had always gone to church as a girl when she lived outside London at Wych Cottage. Val had long ago refused to go to church. He dared not be seen going there by Shorty and his gang. To be dubbed religious would have doomed him to yet fiercer persecution. Doreen took Len to Sunday school regularly, and they came back with stamps stuck in a book. These entitled them to the summer school treat and Christmas party.

The Rector arrived on the second Thursday in February,

looking thin and tired as usual. But his mind was running on a subject that he had been considering the whole week; the idea that good and evil do finally merge and both become a whole that is the will of God. This would help to account for the presence of pain and sin in the world. The Rector started to talk to the rows of girls about it, and he might as well have been addressing them in Greek. Yet they sat and listened to him quite happily, because his goodness and kindness came over to them in spite of his words, and not because of them. Even the teachers looked puzzled, except for Miss Fleetwood, who seemed to know what he was talking about.

After the school had shouted the closing hymn, which was *Fight the Good Fight* and one of the favourites, the Rector seemed to be collecting himself to give out an anouncement.

'We are going to act a play in the church during May,' he said. 'It will be a sort of pageant about the things I have been telling you this morning. There will be martyrs and saints in the play and a lot of ordinary sinners as well, I thought some of you might like to act in it. If so, please give your names to Miss Wilson. Good morning. . . .'

When the Rector had drifted vaguely away, his fine hands clasping a couple of exercise books that he had picked up by mistake, the school was allowed to dismiss for break. The girls all rushed into the cloakroom to discuss the play.

'You going to be in it?' Lou asked Ally. 'I can just see you and me in haloes.' And she began to giggle wildly.

'Bags I being one of the sinners,' shouted Annie Bragg. 'Bring on my hoofs and tail!'

'You won't need any dressing for that part,' yelled Lou, giving Annie a poke.

'Here, who are you pushing?' screamed Annie, poking back.

'Shut up all of you,' Ally cried crossly and she gave both the girls such a shove that they went reeling against the coats on the wall.

Most people spoilt everything by opening their big mouths, thought Ally. Just during the service, while the Rector had been talking, she had had a vague sense of what it was all about. For a second she had caught a glimpse of that strange, mysterious secret, the thing for which she searched. She had decided then to be in the play. Perhaps rehearsing day after day in the church, she would get some clue.

She went out into the noisy, ugly playground, where the girls were eating biscuits and playing catch. The plane tree was in bud and even here in the concrete yard there was a smell of warmth and the reawakening earth. Ally looked at the great tree rising out of the hard, grey paving. The warmth of the sun comforted her, and she felt a rising sense of excitement right through her body. The sun shining down into the crowded yard seemed to promise that one day she would know the greatest secret of all.

Chapter 6

HOME BY SMOG

AT the end of February a week of smog set in. It was horrid waking in the mornings to see everything as dark as night. It grew slightly lighter towards midday but closed in again as soon as school was over. The flats were shrouded in an everlasting veil of blackness that was both damp and sinister. Each street lamp had to fight to make even the smallest glow through the thick blanket of sooty vapour. Each mouthful of air was concentrated coal dust. The children's faces grew pale and streaked with black.

Val grew to hate coming home at night. In the fog, Shorty's gang might be anywhere; in the arches beneath the stairs, waiting on the landings, ambushed behind the bicycle sheds. They had a real down on Val now because they resented a rival gang. Shorty's lot were much heavier and older and Nap, Shorty's second in command, was six feet tall and made like a bull. He had just about as much brain as that animal, but if he fell on you, it was like fighting a tiger. They said in the flats that Nap would kill someone one day, and it was no use arguing with him, because he'd no brains to reason with. He could not even read or write. Blows were all he understood. Then there was Slim Jim who never fought, but who sneaked about spying for the rest. But Thompson was perhaps the most vicious of them all. He had a pinch like a crab, and would come up secretly behind a chap and leave a bruise on him that took days to fade. Shorty did not do much of his own dirty work. He was too clever for that, and the police had never laid hands on him yet, though they had promised Nap Borstal next time he was caught fighting.

Val came across the yard in the yellow haze that he wished was even thicker. He had a scarf over his mouth to keep out the cold vapour, and his hands and wrists were scarlet from the cold. To approach the flats on such a night was like attacking a fortress. He never knew whether it was defended or not; but on this particular evening, he guessed that Shorty's lot might be about. He knew they had sworn to liquidate his own gang.

He kept well away from the bicycle sheds and saw with relief that two women were chatting at the bottom of his stairs. That meant the first danger point was easy. There could be no one hiding in the dark space beneath the stairs. Val ducked round the women while they went on talking.

He dashed up the first flight, braced at any moment for a kick from the shadows or one of Nap's famous springs. Perhaps most of all he feared Thompson. Mum always said Thompson would come to a bad end. Val hoped he would. At the moment he did not feel a debonair gangster any more, but a frightened, hungry boy who was up against heavy odds. Against the darkness, he could imagine Thompson's weasly face with its long nose, and Thompson's thin, pinching fingers stretched out viciously.

There was no one on the first landing except some children with roller skates making a noise. A man looked round a door and yelled, 'Shut that row. I want a nap.' With the man there also volumed out a cloud of radio music. Then the door banged, cutting off the tune. The children ran off past Val, still shrieking.

Second flight. There was a dark corner on the hall landing that might conceal anything. Keeping near to the banisters, Val was up and past it like a shadow. Not a soul on the next corridor, only a couple of tea towels drying that gave Val a start as he thought they were blank, white faces.

The light had fused on the third staircase, he remembered suddenly. So that flight might be the worst place of all. If he succeeded in passing there, he might be all right. Going up silently on the tips of his toes, and keeping well clear of the wall, Val could smell kippers. He thought enviously of the lucky adults who could come home to their tea without having to run the gauntlet every night. He wished that he was fully grown and able to walk about without fear. I'd show that lot then, he thought, and imagined the joy of flattening Shorty's nose.

He felt a prickle of fear in his own nose as he rounded the unlit corner. He stretched out his hands. Nothing. He was almost up. Safe. One more flight to home.

He took the last lot of stairs at a gallop, and so fell right into Thompson's arms. Luckily Thompson was not looking for trouble. He was all cleaned up and going out to the pictures or the pin tables, but Val was taking no chances. Although paralysed by fright, he thought fast, ducked low, clasped Thompson's ankles in their brilliant socks, and brought him down.

Thompson gave a yell as he toppled, and for a few seconds he went bumping sideways across the steps of the ill-lit stairway. Somehow Val got to his feet and bolted along the balcony to his flat. In a moment, unless Thompson was really hurt, he would be up and after his attacker. Val hoped Mum would open the door quickly.

He banged hard at 49. They were in, for the light showed beneath the door. 'Mum,' he yelled, 'let me in.' He knew she was pottering about the kitchen. 'Mum, quick!' At any second Thompson would appear round the stairwell. He would not let such an incident pass without vengeance. 'Mum!' Val banged louder.

When she opened the door, he fell in on top of her.

'Can't you wait a minute?' she asked quite crossly. 'You aren't the fire brigade.'

There was a lovely smell of frying onion. Val drew in a deep breath. He was back in his fortress, the drawbridge up behind him. He was safe. Tomorrow's battle must look after itself. 'What's for tea?' he asked.

He put on his swagger again as he went into the living-room. He was the brigand safe in his mountain cave, the gangster back in his hide-out. No one, not even his family, knew about this guerilla war in which he was permanently engaged. Everybody blamed Val for fighting, but the adults could not guess that it was in self-defence. Once weaken, once give in, and Shorty's lot would slay him. Any unprovoked attacks launched by Val were only to keep up face. Sometimes, in the small hours, he wished he could go and live in a quiet peaceful place. That was why he wanted a bike so badly. On a bike he would be able to escape.

'Going out?' Mum asked him later when he had bolted his mince and onions and three slices of bread and syrup.

'No. Want to see TV.'

He was not risking those stairs again that night.

Chapter 7

THE EPIDEMIC

AFTER the smog came heavy rain, and the whole yard was awash with running water. The small children adored the deluge, especially those who had gum boots and could paddle in the streams. But the mothers cursed it, for they could not dry the washing, and all the flats were steamy with damp clothes. Mum went shopping and got soaked to the skin, and started a cold that turned into flu.

After that the whole of Magnolia Buildings had flu. It was like the Black Death in the history book. One minute you were quite well, and the next in bed with a high temperature. Mum and Val and Ally were all in bed at the same time with sore throats and fever. It was Dad who stayed at home and nursed them all, because Auntie Glad never thought of offering and no one liked to ask her. She just went out to business as usual, did not seem to recognize a family crisis when she saw one, and left Doreen to do all the shopping.

Mum was just out of bed on wobbly legs, and Ally was being allowed to sit up for an hour, when Len got ill.

'I don't like the look of Len,' said Mum to Dad at tea time. 'He says it hurts him to breathe. I've been round trying to borrow a thermometer. We haven't got one, and Mrs Fisher's Jim bit theirs in half.'

'Keep him warm,' said Dad. But when he got back from the Cock later, he didn't like the look of Len either. The child was very red in the face now, and breathing with a queer noise.

'You sleep in with Val,' said Mum to Dad. 'I'll take Lennie with me, I think we ought to get the doctor.'

'It's Sunday tomorrow,' said Dad. 'You won't get the doctor to come on Sunday, especially with him being run off his legs with this epidemic.'

'He's got to come,' cried Mum. 'What do we pay for?' But they put off ringing that night.

Ally never forgot that Sunday. They finally sent her out to telephone on Sunday evening. All the doctor's wife said was, 'He's out. Why didn't you ring up before ten this morning?'

'We didn't know Len was so ill this morning,' argued Ally. 'And we didn't want to bother the doctor on a Sunday.'

'Well, he's out now. I'll give him your message,' said the doctor's wife, who sounded as if she had had enough of the epidemic.

Ally went running home in a state of despair. She always did any telephoning for the family, because nothing would induce Mum to pick up a receiver. She had an idea she might get a shock from it, especially if there should be a thunder storm.

'He won't come,' Ally cried, bursting into the flat. 'Mrs James said we should have rung this morning.'

'I'm sure I don't know,' said Mum, and she went back to look at Len. His face had gone quite pale now and when he woke, he cried. 'I'm sure he's got something worse than flu.'

When Mrs Crawley looked in from next door, she had a look at Len too. 'He ought to have penicillin,' she said. 'I'd say he's got pneumonia. He's breathing just like Bob did before he died.'

Mum looked at Dad. 'You go round to the doctor yourself, Alf,' she said. 'He might come if you went round. We just can't wait until morning.'

But at that very moment there was a knock at the door, and the doctor had arrived. He looked dead tired and was panting from the long climb upstairs. 'Why didn't you let me know this morning?' he asked, but Mum and Dad were too worried to explain. They just took him right in to see Len.

He sat down beside the bed, and said in a cheerful, quite different voice, 'Well, young man, and what's the matter with you?' so that Len who was always polite, tried to smile.

While the doctor was sounding Len and listening to his

breathing, Auntie Glad came back. She asked no questions, but went straight to the scullery, and put on a kettle for her tea, got out a little tray, arranged her own rosy cup and saucer, some milk and sugar. Out of her black bag, she drew a packet of biscuits. When she went into the scullery to wet the teapot, Mrs Crawley who was still there said, 'Chatty, isn't she?' and made her way to the door. As she passed the scullery, she said to Auntie Glad, 'Len's real bad. The doctor's here.'

Auntie Glad did not turn round, but went on making her tea. So Mrs Crawley left the flat.

As Auntie Glad put her tray down on the table, the doctor appeared from Len's room. He was followed by Mum and Dad, and all three looked very grave.

The doctor rummaged in his black bag, and said: 'Give him one of these every four hours, Mrs Berners. Have you an alarm clock? He must not miss a dose all through the night. I'll look in tomorrow morning.'

'What's he got?' asked Mum, and her lips were trembling.

'Just a touch of pleurisy,' said the doctor. 'But don't worry, we'll pull him through. Modern science is wonderful.'

When the doctor had gone, Mum, the usually cheerful, suddenly flopped into a chair and the tears rolled down her cheeks. 'Oh Len! my little chap.'

Dad went across to her and awkwardly patted her on the shoulder. 'He'll be all right,' he mumbled. 'You see! Give him one of the pills.'

During the next few days, each time Ally went out on an errand, she was afraid to come home for fear of what might have happened in the flat. Len lay so quiet, so good, his little crew-cut head only turning uneasily on the pillow.

'He's going to be all right, Mum?' she asked as they both stood outside the bedroom door.

'He's got to be.' Mum would answer fiercely. Her eyes were red-rimmed from no sleep and from weeping. Dad still went to work, but looked home at dinner time. When he was in the flat he moved stealthily as though afraid of disturbing Len.

On the third day, Len asked for a bit of bread and butter. The fever that had sprung on him like a tiger, and that had only been kept down by drugs, now gave up its attack. By the fourth day, Len could sit up and read the comics that Auntie Glad had been keeping for him in case he ever needed them.

All the family sat on the edge of Mum's bed, looking at Len and laughing about the pranks of Dennis the Menace and Beryl the Peril. They felt deeply thankful. Like soldiers after a long, hard fought battle, they were exhausted but happy. For a time the Berners stayed together in the flat, not wanting to go far afield, only anxious to be certain that they were all safe and together.

It was a wonderful day when Len could be carried into the living-room, to sit in the big arm chair. His eyes that seemed too big for his face, were even larger when he saw the great cake Mum had baked. On its white iced top, in pink sugar, was piped the legend 'Get well quick, Len'. Mum cut the cake and everybody had a huge slice, including Mrs Crawley and Mrs Doherty who came in to visit the invalid.

'I'm going to have a pair of roller skates for my birthday,' said Len. His face was all smiles as he bit into his cake.

Chapter 8

WYCH COTTAGE

IT was getting on for spring now and the Common was really coming to life. The prams with all the mothers were out in full force, being pushed about or parked beneath the trees round the bandstand. The old men had brought along their chess or dominoes and were playing serious games, while up above the chestnut leaves shook free from their sheaths, which fell upon the chequered boards. Soon the white and pink flowers would be in bloom. The pigeons made a tremendous cooing, sparrows dive-bombed on to crumbs thrown by the mothers, and the old duck built her nest as usual on the island of the small pond. All over the big pond, white sails sped by, or radio-controlled steamers swept round in wide circles. Cricket was replacing football in the fields, but fat school girls in shorts were still

leaping about the netball courts. Children ran along, tugging at their kites which floated high on the equinoctial winds. There was a tremendous activity too across in the playground where children were swinging, riding, sliding and digging. The cross lady who ran the playground was always pouncing out of her lair to scold boys who mucked about and threw sand in each other's eyes. 'Wouldn't have her job for a thousand pounds,' said all the mothers. In the little wood up by the hard tennis courts, the grass was springing anew, a wonderful brilliant emerald, the bird cherries were out and the may bushes were in bud. Here the lovers strolled or kissed on benches, and the children ran through the wood to see whether the caravans of the May fair had arrived yet, or wandered along to watch the workmen bulldozing the ground where the prefabs had stood. In every single corner of the Common something was happening.

Mum and Dad hardly ever got away from the flats or the streets around the Common, except to go to work. Dad went down to the railway which was about a mile away towards the river, and when Mum was working, she went along the South Bank by bus every morning to clean her office. In the evenings, Dad got as far as the Cock for a half pint of beer, and a chat with his friends, but Mum did not even have that change. By the time she had got tea, washed up, done the ironing, sewn on a few buttons and sent the children to bed, she was thankful to go to bed herself.

So it was a tremendous event for her when she went two or three times a year to see her parents who had a little market garden just outside London. Sometimes, if she went on a Saturday, she would take one of the children to show off to Grandma, but that doubled the fare there and back and could not be thought of very often.

It was after Len had recovered, and while Mum was still at home, that she and Ally went down to Wych Cottage together. Wych Cottage was the name of Grandpa's house. Mum had been looking so tired all the week that Ally was afraid she would not be able to go, and she kept glancing at Mum wondering how she was, and whether the treat would be put off.

'It's no good looking at me every two minutes, Glory,' said Mum a bit sharply, 'because I'm not sugar and won't melt before Saturday.'

'We really are going then?'

'Of course. And you'd better wash your hair and best gloves, and see to your stockings. And mind, Glory, I'm not taking you down there looking like something off the halls. It's all right for round here but Grandma wouldn't like it. You'll wear a skirt – or else!'

There was a tremendous bustle in the flat on Friday night, what with Mum and Ally both washing their hair and putting it into pins. Mum, scarlet in the face, knelt before the electric fire, giving Doreen directions about the warming up of a huge pie that was already made.

'I'll set the oven before I go, see, and don't you go monkeying with it. Then there's only the potatoes to boil, and even you, Doreen Berners, can get around to that.' (Doreen was notoriously undomesticated.) 'Though,' went on Mum, 'I pity the man you marry and that's flat.'

'I'm not going to marry,' said Doreen sulkily, because she was jealous of Ally going to see the grandparents. 'Mum, I've never been to Wych for ever so long.'

'You was sick on the bus last time,' said Mum, rolling over to dry the other side of her head. 'Cor, what a carry on! All over an old gent's trousers.'

'Well, I'm older now,' protested Doreen.

'That don't mean your stomach's less queasy. Look at the Eleven Plus! No, Dor, I'm not risking you on any more coaches. Why, he said he'd send me the cleaner's bill and all.'

'Did he?' asked Len, very interested, bobbing his crew cut up from the comic he was reading.

Mum roared with laughter. 'Of course not. Think I'd give him my address? Not likely!'

'If you get taken queer, aim for the window, Ally,' said Val.

Ally put all her clothes out on her chair that night, so as to be ready for the morning; her best duffle coat, her brown frock, clean petticoat, stockings, gloves, and well polished shoes. The coach went from the Cock at ten, so there was no time to waste. Dad was still laid off on Saturdays, so he would be there to see after Len and the dinner.

It was the first real spring day as Mum and Ally walked over the Common. The grass smelt of new growth, birds were singing, and the sun was actually shining. It seemed like a miracle after the long dark of the winter. No Eskimo seeing the first spring light could have felt more joy than did Ally as she boarded the coach.

It was a nice coach with springy, comfortable seats. Mum

said, 'You can sit by the window, Glory, and look at the view, because it's wasted on me, I always doze off.'

But Ally didn't shut her eyes for a single minute of the way, for it was so seldom that she went any distance from home. As the coach rolled along the suburban streets, she sucked the sweets she had brought for the journey, and rejoiced at everything: the glossy facades of all the Woolworths, the glimpses of cotton frocks in the windows, flowers on the stalls, handsome policemen at crossings, and grand Rolls-Royces with superior looking people in them. She thought a bit about Izzy Waters and wondered what he would think of the rave letters she had written to him, asking for his autograph. When she listened to Izzy on the radio, it seemed as though her bones turned to water.

'Yes, this is a bit of all right. Off my legs and nothing to do,' said Mum, and her eyes shut and her head rolled sideways against Ally's shoulder. In spite of her frizzed-up hair and her lipstick, Mum did look rather grey and tired when she fell asleep.

The coach rolled on and on until it stopped at Wychwood village post office. Mum and Ally, a little stiff, got out, feeling like explorers who had arrived in some distant and savage land. Ally thought of Wychwood as deepest country, because she had never lived outside London, had never left it except to go for a day to the sea. To tell the truth, the village was almost suburban. It might be fifteen miles from Hyde Park Corner, but the town was reaching bungalow arms towards it.

Mum, in her maroon coat and hat to match, led the way, walking uneasily on her high heels along the rough lane that led to Wych Cottage. Ally hopped along beside her, looking for once a neat schoolgirl in a skirt.

The lane wound along between cottages, some old and some new, until right at its rutty end stood a really old cottage with a thatched roof and black beams that shored up the walls of the ancient cob. Around this cottage was a pretty front garden of spring flowers and at the back stretched the market garden, planted in rows with early vegetables, all as neat and patterned as a sampler. An early double cherry tree was in bloom before the door, and a black cat sat on the stone coping of the rough wall, which was tufted with yellow alyssum.

'Cor! Isn't it lovely?' cried Ally. 'I'd forgotten how nice it was.' And she gave a sort of spring into the air from sheer excitement.

'You mind your manners,' said Mum, nervously, pushing a lock of her hair into the maroon felt hat. 'And wait till you're offered things.'

They opened the little gate and walked up the flagged path to the cottage. Grandma opened the door. She looked just as she always did in her neat, violet cardigan, and black skirt with a large white apron over it. Her thin grey hair was drawn smoothly back into a bun; but she did not seem like a real old lady because she was so upright and so on the spot.

'Wipe your feet well,' she said, 'and come in. Well, Marjorie,' she kissed Mum, and then surveyed Ally. 'My, how Gloria grows! She's almost a young woman. Though why you couldn't have taken and called her Mary or Kate or some sensible name, I don't know. Gloria!' she sniffed. 'It's enough to give the girl ideas.'

Mum laughed. 'Don't worry. She's got them.'

'There's a cup of tea waiting.' Grandma led the way in. 'I thought you'd be glad of one.'

Mum, who was a great reader of the women's magazines that the typists threw away in the office wastepaper baskets, had done up her kitchen in the newest way. She had pasted two different wallpapers on her four walls, and had bought curtains of yet another pattern so that the room though bright had a rather kaleidoscopic effect. But Grandma's kitchen seemed to have no particular colour at all. Everything in it had become aged and smoked together, for the perpetual wood haze from the open hearth had lent the same patina to the picture of Queen Alexandra in her coronation robes as it did to the patchwork cushions, the rag rugs, and the faded curtains at the windows. No one had ever modernized Wych Cottage. The floors were still of uneven cobblestones, the fireplace was a huge cavern, the two windows were small and deeply set in the thick walls and had geraniums on their sills that shut out most of the light. Every inch of wall space was covered with pictures and plates made of broken china glued on in patterns. The dresser shelves were a real museum of little ornaments: crested ware from every town Grandma had visited, Victorian figures, parts of dinner sets, odd jugs, pincushions, photographs. But best of all was a walking stick of twisted glass that was filled with millions of hundred and thousand sweets, pink and white. Ever since she was a baby, Ally had longed to possess that walking stick.

After Grandma had asked about the health of the whole family, she exchanged a glance with Mum and said to Ally, 'Now you run along, miss, and find your Grandpa, and tell him that his cup of tea will be ready in ten minutes.'

Ally knew that Grandma wanted to have a talk with Mum, so she jumped up and ran out through the dark little scullery where Grandma cooked on a rusty old oil stove, and out into the big garden at the back.

It was a real pleasure to walk through such a nice, tidy garden where the lettuces were coming up like tiny rosettes, and all sorts of fat buds were sprouting out of the freshly turned earth. Already the apple trees were swelling into pink, tight clusters, and Grandpa had grown them as espaliers that bordered the paths. In other places there were low clipped hedges of box. A long way off, Ally could see Grandpa working in the garden, his old brown clothes merging with the soil. A row of poplar trees made a background and marked the boundary of his land. On either side of the garden, ploughed fields just showed a baby's hair growth of new, green corn.

'Why, if it ain't our Glory!' declared Grandpa, and he gave her a kiss that smelt of earth and tobacco. He was a shrunken, stiffened old man, but his face was rosy and he was always smiling and sunny. It was from him that Mum had got her gay temperament to pass on to Ally. 'Why ain't you been to see your old Granfer before?' he asked. 'There, you'm coming up a proper 'andsome l'il maid. The boys'll be after ye like bees after honey.' He pinched her arm. His voice still had a West Country burr, for he had come from Devon to work as gardener at a big house in Sussex where Grandma had been nurse.

'They said to tell you that tea'll be ready in ten minutes,' said Ally, suddenly realizing all over again how much she liked her grandfather.

The old man winked. 'That's to say as they women don't want you and me for a bit, 'cos they'm talking their heads off. Come along. I'll show you the place a bit, and pick you a nice bunch of they polys over there.'

So Grandpa and Ally slowly promenaded the garden paths, and he pointed out to her what the horrible slugs had done, and told her about greenfly and other pests, so that Ally was quite amazed to know the country harboured so many wicked creatures.

'In town, there's only fleas and flies,' she said.

'I'd lie down and die right away, if I had to live in a dirty old town,' said Grandpa.

When they got back to the house, Mum and Grandma must have had their talk, for they were sitting back, cups in hand, on either side of the hearth, all ready to greet the other two.

'Did you wipe your feet and shut the back door?' asked Grandma.

Ally said she had, and sat down in a small, armless chair by the hearth, feeling she was a story-book character, and not at all the Glory Alleluia of the flats. Grandma somehow produced a compulsion of good manners. Yet it seemed that she had never been able to stop Grandpa from pouring his hot tea into the saucer, and sucking it from the saucer into his bushy grey moustache.

'I've been hearing all the news,' Grandma told the old man.

'Nothing much don't happen here,' he replied.

While the grown-ups talked, Ally looked about her and wondered why she liked the cottage so much. It seemed to have been there for ever and ever, and it was as if Grandma and Grandpa could not live anywhere else. In the flats people were always moving and changing, but perhaps that was because they had not got a piece of real ground under them. I think if I grew some flowers of my own, thought Ally, I would never want to go away and leave them. It's so quiet too, no shouting and bawling like in the flats. I would like to live here.

Before dinner, Grandma took her visitors upstairs to get tidy. The bedroom ceiling was very low, and the window was at floor level so as to squeeze beneath the thatch. There was a large brass bed covered with a white honeycomb quilt. On the walls were texts in frames made of crossed straw.

Grandma had brought up a brass can of hot water so that Mum and Ally could wash in the basin with roses round it. There was no washing in the scullery at Wych Cottage.

They had a very good dinner; stuffed pork, and some of the vegetables from the garden, an apple tart and cream and then more strong tea. When they could eat no more, and were sitting back to digest before attempting to wash up, Ally ventured to ask about the glass walking stick.

'I gave it to your Grandma,' said the old gardener, smiling all over his wrinkled face. 'I bought it at the May fair.'

Suddenly Grandma laughed too, and her prim mouth relaxed and she looked almost young for a moment. 'That was when I was nurse at the Hall,' she said.

'Go on, tell Glory the story,' cried Mum, who was looking better after her meal and rest. 'I used to love it when I was a little girl.'

Grandma preened herself and began. 'I was under nurse there, just at the time of the coronation. There were four young ladies and gentlemen in the family: Miss Olivia, Miss Caroline, and the two boys, Master Gerald and Master Anthony. Master Gerald is Sir Gerald now, but Master Tony was killed in the last war. We had the nicest nurseries, but mind you Nanna, the head nurse, she was a tartar to make a girl work. Up at six I was every morning, and if the whole place wasn't a picture before breakfast, then I knew about it. Then there were the children to wash and dress, for they had to have their breakfast at eight and be downstairs all tidy for prayers at a quarter to nine. I had to put on my clean apron too, and comb my hair and go down with them. After that we went for a walk in the grounds. Oh, you ought to have seen those gardens, the roses and pinks! It took you an hour to walk round all the greenhouses, not that the children were allowed in them.'

'Took us half a day to finish the watering,' said Grandpa.

'Well, the older children had their midday dinner in the dining-room, but I had to carry the heavy trays upstairs to the nursery for the rest of us. The children had a lie down then, and we went for another walk. After tea I had to help Nanna change the young ladies into their white muslin dresses and blue sashes, and the young gentlemen had velveteen suits with lace collars. Pretty as a picture they were, just like those children up there.' And the old lady pointed to a group of Edwardian children patting a dog. The picture had come out of some ancient magazine. 'At five fifteen sharp, Nanna took them downstairs to the drawing-room to be read to by their mamma, but I had my ironing to do . . .'

She sighed, thinking of the days in the great house, while Ally stared at her, fascinated by this peep into so antique a world. 'What happened to the two girls?' she asked, for surely something very glamorous must have happened to them, brought up like that.

'Miss Olivia never married. She writes to me at Christmas,' said Grandma. 'Pretty she was. I never thought she'd be an old maid. Miss Caroline, oh, she had such lovely curls, well, she married a nice gentleman, a banker, and she had three children. But I don't know where she is now.'

'And the glass walking stick?' asked Ally, remembering it suddenly.

'Well, of course, in those days we maids weren't supposed to have followers.'

Mum laughed. 'But you did?'

'Well,' Grandma smiled reminiscently. 'They had to let the gardeners into the house, to bring the fruit and such, though Nanna would have half skinned us girls, if she'd seen us talking to them. Still, I did get to know him.' She nodded at her husband.

'You'll never keep young love apart,' said Mum sentimentally.

Grandpa chuckled. 'Your Grandma was a pretty maid. I sung in the choir in them days, and I used to see all they servant girls coming into church. They had to sit in the pew behind her ladyship, and she'd turn round sermon time to count if they was all there. Plain black hats the girls had to wear, not a flower in them, for all her ladyship was so fond of real flowers in the garden. Still, black hat and all, I noticed your Grandma, and we had a talk or two in the shrubbery. If old Green, the head gardener, had seen us, there'd have been the devil to pay.' The old man chuckled again.

'But what about the next generation?' cried Mum with feeling. 'How did they expect you to get married if you weren't allowed to walk out?'

Grandpa nodded his head. 'Well,' he said, 'neither old Green nor the gentry could stop the fair coming to the town, and that being Gertie's day off, I met her there.'

Grandma gave the fire a poke. 'Marched up to me as bold as brass, and asked me to go for a ride on the horses. The very idea!'

'And did you?' Ally asked eagerly.

'She did, but that was later,' said Grandpa. 'That was after us saw the glass walking stick. I said to her, "Now, me maid . . ." '

'That'll do,' put in Grandma quickly, with a toss of her head, but her cheekbones had gone quite pink.

'Anyway, I bought her the walking stick, though she told me not to.'

'Well, how was I to carry it home? First thing Nanna would have asked was where I got the thing.'

'So then we had our fortunes told.'

'Now Bert, that's quite enough,' said Grandma.

'And do you know what that there fortune teller said,' went on Grandpa with a wicked glint in his eyes. 'Her said to Gertie, "You've a young man what rides a high horse". And that was the first I knew that your Grandma was keeping company with our groom.'

'I never kept company with him,' Grandma protested.

'A silly young chap, he was, thought the world of hisself. Now the fortune teller, a real gipsy she was, with gold rings to her ears, she says to your Grandma, "Yes, me maid, you've got a young man what rides a high horse, but you'll ride the high horse with him, and the two of you'll never marry. The man you marry will take a big stick to you." "No, he won't," cried your Grandma. "No man'll ever beat me." "Won't he then?" says I, and with that, I ups and whacks her with the glass walking stick that her'd forgotten all about. We didn't half laugh, the gipsy and all. So when the old estate carpenter died that spring, I got his cottage and we was married and lived there till we moved here to better ourselves.'

On the way home in the coach, Mum asked, 'Enjoyed your day?'

'Oh, yes,' cried Ally. 'You know, Mum, I sort of wish I'd lived in Grandma's time. It sounds so romantic, not even allowed to meet your true love and all.'

'It was hard work and low pay,' said Mum. 'But there's something I've got to tell you, Glory. I waited till I saw Grandma, but you'll have to know sometime. I'm going in to have an operation next month, so you and Dad'll have to manage somehow. I kept putting it off and putting it off, but now the doctor's booked me a bed at St Michael's.'

'Oh, Mum!' cried Ally feeling that the bottom had dropped out of her world. 'How long'll you be away?'

'A fortnight in the hospital, and then a spell in the convalescent home. Still, I know you'll do your best, and Dad'll lend a hand.'

'You're going to be all right, aren't you, Mum?' Ally asked with a sudden pang of horror.

'Of course I am. It's nothing serious. I'll be as right as rain,' cried Mum, and she gave her old, cheerful laugh.

Chapter 9

VAL'S PERFECT CRIME

'I'VE just got to have a bike,' said Val to himself during the first week of the Easter holidays. 'If I had a bike I could get out of this dump and away from Shorty's gang and go fishing and exploring, and see the world.'

But the question was, how to get the money? Now Mum was not working, cash was shorter than usual. There had been no pocket money at all lately.

Val thought hard as to how he could make money. It was bad luck that it wasn't Guy Fawkes week or carol singing time. You couldn't stand about the streets yelling, 'Penny for the bike!'.

He tried the newsvendors, but they all had boys. Then he went along to see Mr Copley at the stationer's. But everyone knew Val's reputation.

'You're a bad lad,' said old Mr Copley, looking at him over the top of his spectacles. 'Everyone says so. Always fighting!'

'I don't want to fight,' muttered Val, standing sideways to hide a black eye that was fading all too slowly.

'Then why do you do it?' asked the old shopman. 'Look at your coat! It's all ripped. And not a button on it. I want a smart lad.'

Val turned up his arm. The lining stuck out of the cloth. Mum had practically given up mending for him. 'It's a waste of my time,' she had said. 'You ought to go round painted blue like the savages.'

'If the boy you've got now goes, would you take me on then?' asked Val.

'No. I want a steady boy,' said old Copley and turned away.

Val could not explain that he wanted to be steady, that he hated fighting. No one would have believed him. Then, he was proud, too proud to make excuses for himself. So he rubbed his nose on the back of his hand, and so transferred another smudge of black to his face. Dirt just grew on Val.

Next he tried the grocers and the laundry.

'Don't you want a Saturday boy?' he asked. 'I'll come evenings too.'

But they all declared they had boys, and the laundry woman cried, 'Go home and wash your face before you go asking for a job.'

Val hadn't thought of that, so he stood there, taken aback.

The woman sniggered. 'Tell your Mum to put you in the next bag wash.'

Being laughed at was too much! Val could feel tears pricking in his eyes, so he ran away, with the giggling of the laundry girls still in his ear.

Desperate now, he went back to the flat and really washed his face, but this did not extend to his ears or the area behind them, so that he looked like a Negro who had put on a pink mask. Cleaned up, he went to call on Mrs Crawley and Mrs Doherty and some of the other women and asked them all for errands; but everyone replied, 'Run along, Val, and don't bother me. Last time you did my shopping you broke the eggs, and forgot the bread.'

'I couldn't help about the eggs,' said Val. 'That was Thompson. He tackled me low and everything fell out of the basket.'

But all the housewives were like Mr Copley and wanted a steady boy who did not get involved in fights.

At last he gave up his search for work, and went dawdling out into the yard. It's enough to drive you to crime, he said to himself. 'Tisn't as if I wasn't wanting to earn the money honestly.

He went off across the Common and down the High Street, pressing the buttons B in every telephone booth he passed; but someone else had thought of that. He scrumped an apple off a stall, not because he was hungry but as a revenge on a society that did not want him. He went and looked at the lovely

shining new bicycles in the shop windows. They had four gears, pumps, shining bells, carriers – just everything. Val stood there imagining himself coasting down hills, racing along to the sea. He asked himself why other boys had bikes and he didn't. And he said to himself, 'It's not fair.'

He began to hate everybody, and to feel the whole world was against him. He hated a community that refused to let him even work for a bicycle. Wandering on, he came to the Supermarket where there was a great crowd of people doing their shopping. They were pressed right up against the stalls trying to attract the sellers' attention.

I could bring young Len here to do a bit of scrumping, thought Val. I could stand in front of him, and he could pop the stuff in his pockets without anyone noticing. Then he remembered that Len was now eight, and so liable to be summoned as a person responsible for his own actions. Much as Val hated the world, he did not want to involve his little brother with the police.

While all this was going through his head, he was watching a fat lady in a nylon fur coat. She had collected some bananas and a pineapple and was holding them out to be packaged. For a moment she had put down her purse on the counter amongst a bin of apples. Scarcely thinking, but acting on impulse, Val picked up the purse, pocketed it, and dived away out of the crowd. It was done in a second and he was out of sight before the woman had noticed her loss.

So this was what casual scrumping had led to! Val had thought nothing of pinching a stray apple or a cake, and now here he was stealing money.

Going at a brisk walk, but not really running, he slid into one of the back alleys that ran behind the High Street. The purse was burning in his pocket. He was so scared at what he had done that his mouth was dry and his legs felt weak at the knees. At all costs, he must avoid any tangle with the gang or with the police until he had got safe home and hidden the purse.

As soon as he reached the flat, he locked himself in the lavatory so as to examine the purse in peace. With fingers that trembled, he opened the snap of its inner compartment, and found eight pounds in notes and about eight shillings in silver. Enough money to buy a second-hand bicycle!

He did not feel particularly guilty now that he was safe at home. The lady at the counter had never seen him, and would not be able to describe him. No one else had noticed him, for there was such a crush round the stall. He had really committed the perfect crime.

But while he stood there looking at the money, he realized that there were still complications. He could not go out and buy a bike, for his parents would at once wonder where he had got the money.

What a fool he was! Why hadn't he thought of that before? He left the lavatory, went into his room, and sat down on the bed. He had been a thief and all to no purpose. Then suddenly, he saw what he must do. He would have to pretend to get a job. This would mean he would have to disappear every Saturday, and on most evenings. No one in the family would have the time or energy to check up as to where he went.

It was a nuisance not to be able to get the bike at once, because he would not dare to pretend to earn more than ten or twelve shillings a week. And he might have a job to keep all the cash, for with Mum going away, the family might feel Val should contribute from his earnings. The purse and money must be hidden. A permanently safe hiding place must be found and that would be difficult, for the flat was so small and so overpopulated that it had no secret corners. Val thought of the cellar in the deserted house, but that was a long way off and the other boys might find his treasure there, or the house breakers or builders might take possession at any moment. It would not be safe to walk about with eight pounds on him. For the first time, Val discovered the problem of the safe keeping of wealth. For the time being, he shoved the purse under his mattress. But before he did so, he extricated the odd eight shillings, because it would be nice to buy sweets or cigarettes or even go to the pictures after all these weeks without any pocket money.

No sooner had Val money in his pocket than he wished to show off, to hint to Shorty's lot that he was rich, a chap who really did things, and who didn't care for the police. But it was rather difficult to think how to convey all this.

As he strolled nonchalantly across the yard, he saw Shorty

and Nap smoking by the bicycle sheds. They dared not attack Val, for Sprot and some women were about. Val got clean away and down the road, but as he came to the tobacconist's kiosk, he had a bright idea. Those boys might smoke dull, ordinary fags, but he, Val, would show them! He marched into the tobacconists, and said, 'Dad wants a couple of toofers, please.' Toofers were small black cigars that used to be two for a penny but now cost about a shilling each. Two shillings was well spent if it impressed the other gang. Dad sometimes did buy a toofer for a treat, so the man in the kiosk handed them over to Val without any question.

When Val got to the Common, he started to get his toofer going. He had smoked cigarettes made up from odd stubs and rerolled in lavatory papers, but this toofer, once started burning, was much more pungent. Still, anything to impress Shorty and Nap.

Puffing at his toofer like a steam engine, Val strolled across the yard. The cigar smelt so strong that its blue smoke was wafted over to Nap and Shorty. Val did not want to spoil the effect by lingering, but went right across the yard and up the stairs towards his flat. But as he came to the top flight, he suddenly felt so strange and dizzy that he was forced to sit down on a stair, and the half-smoked toofer fell from his fingers on to to the concrete floor.

Mum found him there as she went out to do her shopping. He was sitting with his head against the wall, his eyes closed and the toofer lay at his feet.

'Cor, Val, whatever . . .?'

He opened his eyes and struggled to rise, but his cheeks were green beneath their layer of dirt.

Then Mum saw the toofer, and asked, 'Where did you get that thing?'

'Someone gave it me.' Even in his last extremity Val could still think.

'Get on!' Mum knew Val well enough to recognize a lie, and with one quick movement, she frisked him. There was a jingle of money as she touched his side, and she plunged her hand into his pocket, crying, 'Where did you get that from?'

Val's brain, fuddled by the toofer, moved slower than usual, and there was quite a perceptible pause before he answered, 'I earned it.'

'Come again!' cried Mum. 'That won't wash! You'll come right back to the flat with me, my lord. I've got one or two things to ask you.'

A group of women had collected below them, waiting to come upstairs. When Mum saw nosey Mrs. Crawley, she yanked Val up by his coat collar, kicked the toofer out of the way, and marched the boy along to 49. Mrs Crawley and Mrs Doherty exchanged amused glances. Really, that Val was a caution!

In the living-room, Mum faced Val. 'Have you been scrumping?'

'No.'

'You have, and don't you lie to me.' She took a step forward, her usually smiling face drawn and worried. 'Where'd you get that money, Val? Give it here. I know Dad and I didn't give you any, so you can't have got it honestly. When I tell your Dad he won't half give you a leathering.'

'Mum! Oh no!' Val put the armchair between himself and Mum, for in spite of her good temper she could be really angry if roused.

'Tell me the truth!' she cried. 'And give me that money. Where did you get it?'

Very slowly and unwillingly, Val produced the money coin by coin. Three shillings, four. He hoped to keep back at least a couple, but Mum went on waiting with outstretched hand until he had disgorged all of the remaining silver. When she had got it, Mum went on with her catechism.

'Where did you get it?'

'I – I found it.'

'Where?'

Val was feeling too sick to think up a good story, so he came out with the truth. 'In the Supermarket.'

'How do you mean, found?'

'It was on a stall.'

'So you've been whipping the change?'

'No, no.' All the time, Val had been edging nearer and nearer to the door, so as to be ready to make a dash for it, if he could distract Mum's attention just for one second. But she was too quick for him. She dodged round to the door herself, and grabbed his wrist.

'Now, I'll have the truth out of you, Val Berners, if I have to beat it out. Whose is this money?'

Val began to redden. 'Someone dropped their purse.'

'That's another lie,' said Mum. 'Where's the purse then?'

Val saw that he had been silly to mention the purse. 'I threw it away,' he said.

'And that's another lie,' said Mum, who was by now very angry indeed, angry and horrified to find out that her son was a thief. She grabbed hold of Val, crying, 'You give me that purse at once.'

Val fought and struggled to get away from her, but Mum held on tight. 'I won't, I can't,' he sobbed, for he could not let go his only chance of a bike.

'Where did you hide it?' Mum shook him hard, and this on top of the toofers finished Val's defiance. 'If you don't tell me, I'll go to the police and have you put away.'

When at last he confessed it was under his mattress, Mum marched straight to the bed and drew out the purse. The line of her mouth was grim.

'You're a thief, a dirty little sneaking thief!' she cried and slapped him hard across the cheek. 'Your Grandpa and Grandma would die of shame if they knew what you'd done. Dad and me's brought you up honest. We never cheated anyone in our lives, and now look at you! Dirty, low cheat!' Mum suddenly collapsed, the anger died out of her and she sank into a chair and began to sob bitterly.

Val stood by, staring at her, horrified. In all his life he had never seen Mum cry before. She had never before slapped his face. Now she had called him a dirty little sneak thief and a cheat, and all his pride was outraged. He had never thought of himself as a thief. His scrumping had just been an adventure, even this taking of the purse was not stealing, but a revenge on people that would not let him earn money. But Mum had said he was a disgrace, a shame to the family. She had called him a thief. He couldn't be that. He wasn't that. But then what was he?

'How could you do it, Val?' Mum was sobbing. 'How could you? I brought you up decent. I've done everything I could to give you clothes and proper food. I got up early and went to work, even when I was ill. And now look what you've done!

It's all been no good.' And she sobbed more bitterly than ever, feeling the whole defeat, the waste of the bad nights during Val's teething, her savings spent on his first little trousers, his pop gun, his school shoes, his summer holiday. All she had done for him was sheer loss if he were to grow up a thief.

By this time, the tears were pouring down Val's cheeks too, making tunnels in the general grime. He turned away from his mother to hide his trembling mouth. He couldn't cry in front of any woman, not even his mother.

'I wanted a bike,' he said. 'All the other boys have got bikes.'

'I'd have given you a bike if I'd had the money,' sobbed Mum. 'You know that, Val. But to steal for it – oh!'

'I didn't want to steal for it,' said Val. 'I tried to get a job, but no one would take me. I asked everywhere.' He was walking about the room, banging unseeingly into the chairs and tables. 'They laughed at me – they said – they said . . . 'and he was weeping too.

Presently they both got calmer.

'I was so proud of you, Val,' said Mum in a sorrowful voice. 'You don't know. And so was Dad. We both thought the world of you.'

Val had to face the devastating thought that his parents would never be so proud of him again.

'I ought to have made you go to Sunday school,' said Mum. 'But I'm always so tired. Val, we've got to take that purse back.'

Val grabbed at her arm. 'No, Mum. They'll send me away. No, we can't take it back.'

'We must.' She got up and scrubbed at her eyes with a tea towel. 'We'll take it to the police and say you picked it up in the Supermarket – on the floor. We'll say that. Go and wash your face, Val. You're coming with me.'

'Oh no, Mum. I can't. They'll guess.'

'You're coming with me, or I'll tell your Dad.'

Val faced her, his countenance blotchy with tears and dirt. 'Suppose the lady doesn't go to the station?'

'We'll tell them at the fruit stall as well. She probably made a fuss there. But we've got to take the purse to the police. We've got to put this right, so you can start again. And Val, this must be the end of thieving, or scrumping which is the same. Take one thing, and you'll take another. And if I ever catch you again I'll hand you over to the police with my own hands, and have you put away. I'm not having any thieves in our family and that's straight.'

They went to the police station and Mum went up to the desk, while Val stood close beside her. He knew a great many of the local cops, and hoped they would not recognize him.

'My boy found this in the Supermarket, by the fruit stall,' said Mum to the officer behind the counter. 'I thought it best to bring it straight here in case the – the person inquires. I'll also let them know at the stall in case she – or he goes there.'

Val thought that the policeman gave him a sharp glance, but all the man did was to check the money in the purse and ask Mum to give him details for the book.

'We'll let you know if it's claimed, ma'am,' said the officer.

'Val,' said Mum as they walked home. 'I've got to go into hospital next week. I shan't get much peace or rest lying there if I'm afraid all the time of you getting into trouble.'

Val kicked a stone along the gutter.

'Suppose Dad came and told me they'd caught you? That you were being sent away, and me not home?'

Val slid his hand into hers, just as he had when he was a small child.

'Val, promise me you won't do it any more?'

He squeezed her hand and they left it at that.

Chapter 10

NIGHTGOWNS

THE chief difficulty about going to hospital was – nightgowns. It might be all right at home to go to bed in petticoats or old summer dresses. But you couldn't wear these sitting up in a ward with all the other ladies in nice ribboned bedjackets, looking as smart as fashion plates. But where was Mum to raise a couple of decent nightgowns, let alone the four the hospital asked for? 'I've got my cardigan I could wear in bed,' Mum said to Ally, 'and I've got one nightgown, but that's all. You know, Glory, I've never had a dressing-jacket. One of those lovely soft, Shetland wool ones with little bows of ribbon. I saw a beauty up at Ladds and Fallow last week.'

When Mrs Crawley heard of Mum's difficulty she promised to lend her one of the nightgowns that she had had for her bad leg the time she went to St Paul's.

'It's ever so good of her,' Mum explained to Ally, 'because if you don't take enough things, they put you into awful old hospital gowns. I'd die of shame rather than wear one of those workhouse outfits.'

Grandma sent on another nightgown, but it must have been made in the reign of Queen Victoria, for it was of the thickest calico, and had long sleeves to the wrists and frills. The whole garment was starched stiff as a board and the frills were offered nicely.

'Cor, I couldn't be seen dead in that thing,' said Mum, holding it up in horror. 'Pity, because it's good as new. Must have been one that her lady gave her when she married.'

'Could we alter it a bit?' said Ally, but she knew that she and Mum would make a mess of such a task. They were both hopeless at sewing.

'I'll take it to needlework class,' piped up Doreen. 'The

teacher'd help me with it.' Doreen was good at sewing and handicrafts.

Mum looked doubtful. 'It'll be like sewing sail cloth.'

The thought of the hospital ward and the other scornful lady patients sent Mum to the post office to draw out thirty shillings of her small savings. With this she bought a peach coloured creation with lace on it.

'And you'll just have to take my things home and wash them up quick,' she said to Ally.

The last evening, Mrs Crawley and Mrs Doherty dropped in to wish Mum luck, and give her plenty of advice about hospital life. Mum's little suitcase was already packed, but it was undone again to show the ladies the new peach nightgown, and the one remodelled by Doreen that had been so blood-stained from pricked fingers, it had had to be relaundered.

'But I did it all myself, didn't I, Mum?' cried Doreen, who was always very anxious for any praise or notice.

While the three women and the girls were chattering ten to the dozen, Dad came home. He carried a brown paper parcel and looked so sheepish that all the ladies couldn't help smiling.

'Brought you something, Marge,' he mumbled and shoved the parcel into her hands and went straight on to the scullery to have his clean off. Mum undid the parcel with fingers that trembled from excitement. Inside, was the very pale blue Shetland wool bedjacket that she had described.

'Cor!' she cried and held it up with delight.

'I told Dad you wanted it!' shouted Ally, dancing about. 'Isn't it lovely?'

'Good old Dad!' screamed Mum, her black eyes sparkling and some colour coming into her pale cheeks. 'There! Now I'll be able to sit up with the other girls and not feel ashamed. Why, it's just like getting married and having a trousseau. Half a minute, Alf Berners, you've got to have a kiss for this, like it or not.' And she ran into the dark little scullery and kissed Dad, who was all wet from washing. 'Fancy you getting your post office money out for me! Oh, you don't know! I'm ever so pleased.'

'And isn't it the sweetest thing?' exclaimed Mrs Doherty in her soft Irish voice, and she held up the filmy wool in her hand. 'And there's myself wishing I could be going to hospital too and sitting up like a fine lady with all the world to serve me. Wait now, till I get ye my sponge bag with roses on it that I had for Christmas. For I've been meaning to lend it ye. There's always a day's march to the bathroom, and ye'll be after needing something to carry your soap and toothbrush.'

'Oh, Mum, what about a dressing gown for going to the bathroom?' Ally had suddenly visualized this need.

Mum looked downcast for a minute. 'Well, I'll just have to wear my maroon coat.'

'Och, there's many of them won't be having a dressing-gown,' cried Mrs Doherty, her blue eyes kind in her worn face.

'And isn't your maroon coat as smart as anything ye'd see around the Common, Mrs Berners, dear.'

'Now, I must put all the things back in the case again,' said Mum. 'Where's my brush and comb? That's all clean. And here's my hankies, and a tin of sweets Ally gave me.' She tucked everything away, as pleased as if she were a young girl going on her first visit.

'We'll all be up to see you, dear,' Mrs Crawley cried as the two women went off to give their families some tea.

The rest of the evening, Mum kept reminding her own family of everything they had to do while she was away: the plants to be watered, Len must go to bed early, Val had to wash, Dad should have a clean vest after his weekly bath.

It was quite late by the time Auntie Glad turned up. She crept round the door as usual, almost invisible in her black coat and hat, ate the supper Mum had kept hot for her, and said nothing about a large parcel she was carrying. Mum chivied all the children off to bed, as they must be astir earlier than usual. Mum had to be at the hospital by ten.

Dad had gone across to the Cock, and Mum was polishing off the last of the ironing, when the little dressmaker produced her parcel without saying a word.

'Oh, Glad! Whatever is it?' Then she cried out: 'Oh!' as if she had been shown a peep of heaven and could not believe it. 'A dressing-gown, a lovely, pink wool dressing-gown! With a quilted collar and all. Glad, where did you get it? It's never for me? Oh, Glad!'

'I made it, see,' explained Auntie Glad in her toneless whisper. 'It was a remnant that Miss S. said I could have for a song. I ran it up in the dinner hours.'

'But it's lovely. It's like a real shop one. Look at its tassel and cord and the way the sleeves are finished. I never had anything like it before. Oh, you are so good to me!' The tears stood in Mum's eyes as she shook the elegant garment out of layers and layers of tissue paper.

'Well, you've been good to me, Marge,' said Auntie Glad.

'There's many wouldn't have took me in, not with your big family. I was glad to do it for you.'

Mum hugged the little woman, and then as Dad came in at that moment she hugged him too, for his bedjacket must not be eclipsed. It had to be unpacked once more to be shown to Auntie Glad.

Mum put on the new dressing-gown and paraded up and down for the children, who got out of bed to see the wonderful garment.

'I'll just run and fetch Mrs Crawley and Mrs Doherty,' said Ally, who was still in trousers and sweater. 'They've got to see it while it's new, and before you upset something on it. You won't have to wear your maroon coat now.'

The Crawley and Doherty families were not yet in bed, and so they came crowding into the small room while Mum did mannequin.

'You'll be the grandest woman in the ward, so you will!' cried Mrs Doherty, 'and may the Virgin bless and keep ye. Now away to bed the lot of ye, for the poor woman will be needing her rest.'

'Don't you worry,' said Mrs Crawley. 'I'll pop in and out and keep an eye on things.'

'There! I never had a nicer evening in my life,' said Mum as she and Dad went off to bed. 'It's almost worth going to hospital to find out how kind people are!'

Dad took her up to St Michael's in the morning. Ally had offered to go, but Dad had said, 'Those flipping British Railways can hang theirselves if I can't look after my wife when she's ill.'

Chapter 11

MUM AWAY

WHEN the operation was safely over and there was an official bulletin saying Mum was going on as well as could be expected, the family relaxed and returned to normal; but the flat did seem very quiet and lifeless without Mum there, laughing and drinking tea and gossiping with her friends.

To begin with, Ally was very conscientious. She got up early and bullied the boys into washing and then cooked breakfast. In the evenings, she hurried home after school to make tea and catch up with the chores. Val and Doreen also tried to help, and even offered to do all the shopping. But after a few days the children got bored with their own virtue. Dad and Auntie Glad had not changed their ways. They just did their own work and did not attempt to help in the flat. Little by little Val slacked off, and soon he and Doreen were leaving all the housework to Ally. Ally would not have minded if she could have dramatized herself as the noble daughter doing her duty by the stricken and motherless household. There could have been glamour in such a role. But for that she needed a proper audience, and the family didn't provide one. They just took all her efforts for granted, never told her how well she was doing, and only grumbled if she wasn't up to Mum's standard.

They all took it for granted that Ally should stay at home every evening, and couldn't act in the church play or go to the pictures. All the other girls at school were in the play and they told Ally about the rehearsals and the exciting costumes they were to wear, so that Ally rapidly developed a grievance.

'Cor! Glamour!' she muttered, as she washed up piles of dirty dishes. No one had stayed to help her in spite of her grumbling. Val just said washing-up was a woman's work and Dad didn't do it. Dad had gone to the Cock as usual on his way to visit Mum. Len was too slow to be much use, and Doreen had insisted she must finish an essay.

'What do you want to do homework for now?' shouted Ally, her heart swelling with a sense of injustice. 'You've done your exam. A rotten bad wife you'll make.'

'I shan't ever marry. I'm not that sort,' said Doreen placidly. 'Now just shut up a mo. I've got to concentrate.'

In her rage, Ally broke a saucer, choked the drain with grease and in trying to clear it, tipped boiling water over her wrist.

The whole flat was running at sixes and sevens. Doreen got sick eating too many sweets, Val stayed out till all hours and Len was always whining and asking for Mum.

Finally, Ally got slack herself. She stopped trying to cook proper meals, and just went out and bought fish and chips. She scarcely cleaned at all, only brushed the dirt under the mats or the beds. Not only laziness made her scamp her work, it was tiredness as well. During the last few months she had been getting fatter, and the girls at school laughed at her and called her Pudding Face. So she had started to diet, giving up bread and potatoes and margarine. As she was not eating enough for her growing body, she grew tireder and tireder, and as she got tired, she became cross and hysterical.

In spite of her constant fatigue, she tried to do exercises, but there was really no space in the small flat, where the rooms were crowded with furniture. She could not even do the exercises on her bed, because Doreen always seemed to be in it.

'Oh, dear, you can't have glamour if you're fat,' Ally kept saying to herself. Her skirts would not fasten, her trousers bulged, and in the evenings she had dizzy fits, and so could not do the mending. The boys shed their buttons as a tree sheds its leaves. Soon all their clothes were gaping and they had scant means of keeping up their trousers.

Until now, Ally had had no idea how many clean clothes were needed by seven people in a week. Mum had told her to take the washing up to the launderette on Saturdays. Ally wheeled it over in the shopping basket, but was horrified to find what a weight the damp things were as she lugged them back up four flights of stairs. Nor did the washing machines do the ironing. The damp clothes lay about in piles, getting grimy all over again, because Ally had not the energy to tackle them. Finally the boys, when they ran out of shirts, pulled them damp and unironed from the pile and wore them like that. It may have been wearing damp clothes, or just the sudden hot weather that gave Len a bad cold. He went round with a streaming nose that nothing would staunch, and whined for Mum more than ever.

As well as all the housework, Ally had to trail up to the hospital every other evening to visit Mum and bring back the nightgowns that had to be properly washed and ironed. Sometimes Ally quite envied her mother, sitting up in bed with the nice new jacket.

Mum was, of course, the life and soul of the ward. Whenever Ally came in, she was exchanging jokes and sallies with all the other patients. She had a quip for every ward maid, doctor or lady in overalls, and she made everyone laugh. If any patient dared to look downcast, Mum would cry, 'Want me to come over and chalk you up a smile with my lipstick?'

Mum knew all about everybody in the ward, what was the matter with them and what the doctor had said. She would pour all this information out to Ally as she sat by the bed. 'See her over there? That's Mrs Hodson. Poor girl, she had a kidney out last Tuesday and her with four lovely kiddies. Next to her, yes, that one with carroty hair, that's Beryl. She's engaged. Ever such a nice young chap comes to see her. See that nurse in the small cap? That's Sister Amory. She doesn't half holler at you. How's my Lennie? Bless him! I wish he was allowed in. Did you water the plants, Glory? Seen anything of Mrs Crawley? Don't you let her poke her nose into everything, or we'll never get it out again. Quick, ducks, tell me all the news, because the bell goes in five minutes.'

The woman Mum and Ally liked best in the whole ward

was Mrs Cobber. She lay very still in the next bed, but she was always smiling and cheerful and the whole ward loved her. No one, not even Mum, knew what her trouble was. The nurses said it was some kind of rheumatism of the spine. Mrs Cobber had been there for weeks having treatment. Mum told Ally that she had two sweet children and their photo was on her locker.

One evening, Mrs Cobber seemed happier than ever. Her eyes were shining, and she said to Ally, 'I'll be going home soon, the doctor says. The pain's better, see, and he doesn't think they'll keep me here much longer. Mum'll come and look after me. Three months I've been in, so I shan't half be glad to get home. Dad's put down the new lino since I went, and he says all the tulips are out. I just can't wait to see the children. I just lie here imagining myself getting a nice cup of tea in my own kitchen.'

After Ally had been to see Mum, she did have slight qualms about the flat. 'I'll give it a proper clean out on Saturday,' she promised herself.

But by the time she had done the shopping and lugged it upstairs, and found a slice of bread and jam for Len, she just collapsed into the armchair and stared at the littered room without enthusiasm. The breakfast things were still on the table, last week's washing was still in an untidy heap, the floor was littered with matches, crumbs, shoes, Len's toys and old newspapers. She knew that the scullery was stacked with dirty supper dishes from yesterday, and that out of all the beds, only Auntie Glad's had been made.

Dad came in at that moment and for the first time he seemed to realize the state of total disorder. Perhaps it was seeing Ally strewn across the armchair so early in the day.

'Be glad when Mum's back,' he remarked.

'So'll I,' said Ally. 'Look at it!'

'Can't you straighten things up a bit?' Dad sat down too. It was a very close, hot day, with the heat more exhausting as it had come so suddenly.

'What's the use?' asked Ally in a hard voice, but not moving

an inch. 'As soon as I get it clean, the boys muck it up again. And no one helps me, not even Doreen. Sits here all this week learning sonnets. Cor! What a time to learn sonnets!' And Ally burst into loud, gulping sobs. She was so very, very tired and so empty and hungry.

'Here, hold on,' said Dad, quite worried. 'Doreen ought to help you. Where's she gone?'

'B-Brownies or B-Bible class or something,' sobbed Ally.

'And that Val. Can't he do a bit of shopping?'

'He'd break half the eggs and forget the bread. No, thank you.'

'What a lot!' said Dad disgustedly. 'What about Auntie Glad?'

'Oh, her! You know what she's like.'

Dad nodded. He did. 'Well, Dor and Val should help you,' was all he found to suggest.

Ally sniffed. 'You tell them,' she said. 'I'm tired of asking. You make them help me.'

Dad sat a moment considering what effect he could have on Val and Doreen. He was used to his wife controlling the family. 'Here, come on,' he said at last with a sense of his own nobility. 'Cheer up, Glory. I'll lend you a hand.'

'You?' said Ally, very much surprised, for Dad had been so spoilt and waited on by Mum, he was never expected to do a thing in the house. Yet now he lumbered round the flat and helped Ally to clear the litter from the tables and to wash up.

'I never had any idea how much Mum does,' he said mournfully as he wiped his way through the pile of crocks.

'Nor did I,' sighed Ally.

That night Glory Alleluia had a strange dream. She dreamt that she was acting a play in a very beautiful garden that was filled with wonderful fruit and flowers. Under the trees stood tall angels, each holding a white lily in his hand. Somehow Ally knew that these lilies were glamours, the secret, special kind. She longed to have one, for the lilies were so shining and white and smelt so lovely. Then an angel came towards her and said, 'This is your glamour, Gloria, this is for you.' But to her horror, she saw that he held out a horrible greyish, greenish thing that had limp leaves and was slowly turning to a black decay.

She did not want to take the repulsive thing, but the angel insisted, and as she took it, the dead glamour changed. It swelled up, grew rosy, expanded into the loveliest lily of them all. Then she woke up.

That night when she went up to see Mum, the ward seemed very quiet. Mum was quiet too, and there was no shouting jokes from bed to bed. As Ally kissed her, she was afraid, and said, 'Aren't you better, Mum?' for her mother looked pale and seemed to have been crying.

All Mum did was to make a little gesture towards Mrs Cobber's bed. It was empty. A clean, white quilt was spread over it, there was a fresh pillow case and the sheet was turned back for a new patient. The bedside locker was bare and had been scrubbed clean.

'Has she gone home?' asked Ally. 'She told me she was going.'

'She went – at three this morning,' said Mum. 'But it wasn't to – to where she thought.'

'You mean? Oh no, Mum!' Ally's own eyes also filled with tears. The new lino and the tulips! And the children! Mrs Cobber would never see them now.

'They sent for her husband and put up the screens,' said Mum, 'and in the morning – she wasn't here any more. It makes you think, Ally.'

It made Ally think too. What was this nonsense called glamour? Suppose that Mum had died, and hers had been the empty bed with the clean counterpane? She went straight home, and tired as she was, she began to clean the flat. The next day she went out and bought a good shoulder of lamb and cooked it with two vegetables. She also ate a large helping of it.

Chapter 12

THE MAY FAIR

'IT'S here!' yelled George across the yard one fine Saturday morning.

'It's never!' shouted back Val. 'Cor, George, let's go over there at once. When did it come?'

'Must've been last night. There wasn't anything yesterday.'

For days the boys had been watching for the May fair that came every year to the Common. The may trees were covered with a thick foam of creamy blossom and their leaves were fresh and brilliant. It was high time for the fair to arrive.

Like magic cities, it had grown up in a night. The great long travelling wagons, and the lorries that carried the bumper cars, switch-backs and horses were arranged in a huge circle on the fair-ground. A spring wind was blowing dust in everybody's eyes, but the work went as smooth routine, the show people assembling the booths and machine as if they were mechanical toys. All the boys from the streets round the Common were there, watching, messing about and getting in the way.

Soon the electricity was linked up, and by evening the whole place leapt into a brilliant riot of noise and light. Thousands of bulbs of different colours sparkled and glittered, outlining the booths; raucous music from electric organs was broadcast from every corner, the different tunes shouting each other down or being split asunder by the screaming sirens of the flying boats.

At the back of the show, in the green dusk, the show people had set up their usual domestic lives, strung their washing to the may trees, and filled their dustbins with rubbish. The babies and dogs played beneath the wagon wheels, while old crones peeled potatoes and stoked the stoves that puffed blue smoke out of the wagon chimneys.

The boys had saved all their pennies for the fair, and each evening they tried to decide between delicious hot dogs that were bedded down in fried onion, or candy floss, pink, synthetic and amusing to eat. It cost a lot of money to ride on the horses or go down the helter-skelter tower, and even more to shoot with rifles at the dancing ping-pong balls. There were great crowds round the shooting booths, but it was a shilling to have a go with one of the rifles that never threw true.

Ally had run into Brian Doherty on the top balcony on Friday evening, and to her surprise, he had said, 'You going to the fair?'

'Is it here?' asked Ally.

'They're putting it up. Like to come and see?'

'Aren't you going with Val and the rest?' Ally saw with surprise how tall Brian was now. He must have grown a lot during the last weeks. 'I can't tonight. Got to go and see Mum. She's off to the convalescent home tomorrow.'

Val, who had no money, went to the fair every evening. He loved the fair and looked forward to it all the year round. At night, when the whole place was absolutely vibrating with noisy music, the warmth, the light, the colour, the cheerfulness and sparkle gave him a tremendous thrill. He longed to be the man who leapt so nonchalantly on and off the bumper cars, or the people who loaded up the rifles and ducked so as not to be shot. Even without a penny he could spend hours there. It was wonderful to trot across the grass of the dark Common, and to see the reflected flare on the tree tops and to hear the drumming, roaring music grow louder and louder. He would wander around for hours, shoving through the crowds, dodging between the booths, and peering into the mysterious darkness at the back where these queer nomadic people lived.

Dad had promised Ally to lecture Val and Doreen about helping with the housework; but Dad had only sunk to bribery, and promised Val a couple of shillings to spend at the fair if he lent a hand with the washing up.

With real money in his pocket, Val went off on Saturday,

full of excitement. The rest of his gang were waiting to go with him and all seven boys went trotting over the dark grass together.

'Tell you what,' said Val. 'Let's all have a ride on the horses, and we could try changing places while they're going round, see. That'd be smashing.'

'I'm going down the tower,' yelled Ginger, who was usually rebellious and cheeky. 'My grannie gave me half a crown.'

'You're not then,' said George as lieutenant to Val. 'You do what we do, see.' And he gave Ginger a sidelong punch as they ran.

But there was no time to stop and fight, for the thumping music called them, and at last they arrived at the entrance to the fair where a man was selling funny hats. Val led the way to the horses, which had just started off on a fresh turn. The gang stood there, waiting, mouths slightly open as they watched the people on crocodiles, swans and Arab steeds sailing round and round and up and down. Everything glittered and shone, the brass poles that went right through the stomachs of the animals, the gaudy pictures, the flowers and the gilt organ. The boys were mesmerized by the glory of it all, when suddenly, they felt a surging of bodies behind them, and heard Nap's voice crying out, 'Look who's here. Those nasty little boys. Get on home, you lot!'

'Oh gosh!' muttered Val, spinning round. Why must they come now and spoil everything? But Nap was already twitching out George's tie and Thompson was hovering, waiting to administer a sharp pinch. To escape the attentions of Shorty's gang, Val yelled, 'They're stopping! Jump on!' For the roundabout had slowed down. Val's gang made a leap on to the animals, clinging to their brass poles, and praying that the mechanism would soon start again.

'Did the little boys ride on their nice horsies,' jeered Thompson, and he and Nap and two others sprang on to the platform that was now slowly revolving. When Val saw a battle was inevitable, he kicked out and caught Shorty on the side of the jaw.

'Dirty play!' yelled Shorty, rubbing his jaw, and then the whole gang closed in, all springing on to the platform and trying to pull the smaller boys off their seats. Thompson attacked George who kicked back and the fight grew fierce. Val's crowd fought as valiantly as any knights on real horses. Nap got hit sideways by a descending swan, and thinking it was George, tugged him off his crocodile. The ordinary public by this time was terrified, especially some girls who screamed like steam whistles. The fighting boys struggled in and around them while the moving animals went on going up and down and round and round. The yelling soon rose above the music, and the man who had been collecting money on the other side of the platform ran along the step and joined in the fight, throwing any loose body off on to the ground. He had yelled at the man in control of the machine, but the man did not hear at first, so the roundabout continued to revolve with figures battling all over it.

Val managed to climb up and stand on his seat, clinging to one of the brass bars while Nap tugged, dragging him down. Each time Nap looked like winning, the horse rose, carrying both boys with it. Val, who was as agile as a monkey, pulled himself free, leapt off and sprang towards a crocodile. He clutched at the girl who was riding it, she toppled and screeched and Val hit his nose, and felt blood spurt forth. The whole roundabout was now a mass of flailing arms and legs. Then abruptly the mechanism stopped, the platform slowed down, and the police closed in.

Val had only one idea, to escape from the cops. He knew that as leader of the gang he should stay and speak up and explain that Shorty's lot had attacked them; but he also knew that the police would not listen. His nose was bleeding, his filthy clothes were ripped. He was in no kind of state to put up a defence. Then, he had promised Mum not to get into trouble while she was in hospital, and if he were caught now, he was certain to be sent to a special school for bad boys.

None of this did he argue out with himself at the time. Escape was just an automatic reflex. In the confusion, the screaming of the women, the shouting of the boys, the roars of police and their whistles, Val dodged between the animals, wriggled out of the clutch of a man who tried to capture him, and was down and off the other side of the roundabout, between two booths and into the trees in a flash. Once in the thicket he did not pause, but kept on running, leaving behind the yells and angry voice that were soon merged into the music of the other machines.

The Common was deserted except for a few strolling lovers, and with a pounding heart, Val somehow made his way back to the flat. His nose was bleeding less now and he mopped it on his sleeve. Oh, to be safe in bed beside Len!

As he ran, several disquieting thoughts attacked him. Suppose the rest of the gang was caught and taken to court, what would they say to a leader that had deserted them? If they were punished and Val got off scot free, might they not all side against him, or even join up with Shorty's lot? If Val were deserted by all his friends, Shorty could soon destroy him.

Running across the grass, all Val knew clearly was that the police must not get him, because that would worry Mum, and make her worse. If Mum died, it would be the end of the world.

When he got to the yard, he walked sedately. He mustn't seem to be hurrying. All the way upstairs the argument went on in his head. If the gang thought him a traitor? But then, even if he had stayed, what could he have done? The police dealing with a large scale fight would not listen to a twelve-year-old boy.

If only Mum were home! It would be no use to go to Dad, because he would never listen to all the ins and outs of the story. He would only be angry that Val had got involved in more trouble, and might even leather him into the bargain.

In the dark, the flats were grim like a fortress. Most of the inhabitants had gone to bed, and the lights were moving from living-room to bedroom. By now, Dad must be back from the Cock. There was still the problem of how to get into the flat without too much inquiry. Ally had been so cross lately. She would be sure to side with the grown-ups if there were a fuss.

Val went up the stairs very quietly, and was about to run along the top balcony, when he almost collided with Mrs Doherty, who had popped out of her door. 'Wait now!' she caught at him. 'Where's Brian?'

'I don't know,' gasped Val. Probably in a police van or even in an ambulance, he thought. The light from the open door showed Mrs Doherty the fear beneath the dirt on Val's face.

'Was he not at the fair with you?'

'We – we got separated, see.' Val tried to wriggle loose. He must get into bed. Only there would he be safe, if the police should come making inquiries. Any of his gang under fierce grilling might betray him. Billy in particular could never keep anything to himself.

'It's late, so it is,' said Mrs Doherty. She had put an old shawl over her head, for the night was turning chilly. 'Were you riding on the roundabouts and such?' At the word roundabout Val must have winced, for Mrs Doherty looked closer, saw blood on his shirt, and grabbed his arm. She had not lived through the Irish rebellion for nothing, and could spot trouble when she saw it.

'Wait now, Val. Something's happened. Tell me the truth of it.'

Val's first instinct was to pull away and run, but then he realized that he must get help. Mrs Doherty was the mother of one of his gang. He must try and make her understand.

'It was Shorty – ' he began. 'Twasn't us.'

'Oh that lot,' breathed the woman. 'Go on.'

'We weren't doing nothing. Honest. Just waiting for the roundabout to stop, and we were going to have a ride, see. Shorty and his crowd came up. They started it all. We didn't want to fight. We were just enjoying ourselves, see. We got up on the horses so as to be out of the way, but they came up after us, and started to hit us and muck us about. They tried to pull us off. All the people were yelling. Then the police came, and I got away.'

'But the police? God save us. What happened to my Brian?'

'I don't know. He hates fighting, but Nap went for him. Shorty's lot are bigger than us.'

'The saints help us! So he may be in the hands of the police.' Mrs Doherty half turned to her door, and then cried, 'And himself's on night duty. And me not able to leave the small creatures.'

'I couldn't do anything,' said Val defensively. 'They wouldn't have listened to me. We didn't start the fight.'

'It's that Shorty. May curses be upon him for a wicked devil!' cried Mrs Doherty. 'Those boy-os are a shame and a plague on this place, so they are. No one has dared raise a hand to them, and it's time they were punished. My Brian's as quiet as a lamb if left to himself, and him with his nose never out of a book, and my sister saying he was fit for the priesthood. It's myself will go to the police and all the other mothers too, for it's enough we've had of their wicked ways. There's no boy walks safe in this block, because of their persecution.'

With the white shawl round her head, Mrs Doherty looked like some wild prophetess. Val stared at her amazed. He had never guessed the parents knew about Shorty's gang. He had just thought of it as an inevitable misery that only affected himself and his friends.

'They always blame me for fighting,' he said bitterly. 'But I don't want to fight. It's them. They start it. I've just got to protect myself.'

'Whisht then. Mrs Crawley'll be putting her nose out, if she hears us. I don't want her noseying about this. If Brian does not come back, I must away to the police station. Were there witnesses up there by the horses?'

'There was plenty of people. But it all started so quick, see.'

'Sometimes I curse the day we left Ireland and came to this wicked city,' wailed Mrs Doherty.

Luckily at this moment, Brian himself appeared; but what a wreck of a Brian it was! The usual quiet, tidy youth was filthy. His clothes were torn, and there was a great gash across his cheek. One eye was black and already closing.

'Brian!' cried his mother. 'Have they killed you?'

'Almost,' said Brian, who had been looking scared, but was now relieved to see Val on good terms with his mother.

'Where's the others?' asked Val.

'They took George, the police did, and Shorty and Thompson. But Nap got away and so did the rest of us. Oh, Mum, it was awful. They just started it. Nap rolled me off my horse and I fell on to the platform, see, and hit my face. It doesn't half hurt.'

'Come in and I'll wash you,' said Mrs. Doherty. 'The Virgin be praised! I thought you were in prison.'

'How did you get away?' Brian asked Val.

'Oh, I slipped off,' said Val, his old manner returning. 'How did they get George?'

'He was underneath Shorty. There wasn't half a row. You

never saw so many cops. Oh, and Ginger's had it. Broke his arm. I saw the ambulance as I got away. It wasn't our fault, Mum.'

'It's myself and some of the other mothers will go to the police tomorrow,' said Mrs Doherty. 'It's the last we'll have of this fighting. Away in now, Brian, love, and we'll put something on your face. One of these days that Nap will kill somebody. You go to bed, Val, or there'll be trouble for you. I wonder if anyone has told Ginger's mother?'

'There's the police car below,' hissed Val suddenly. The black car with its aerial had driven right into the yard, and two policemen were getting out.

'I'm going,' said Val, and he shot along the balcony and knocked on 49. Mrs Doherty and Brian also vanished like rabbits into holes.

Luckily for Val, Ally was up late, as she had washed her hair and was drying it in the new pins prescribed by *Woman and Loveliness*.

'Where've you been?' she asked angrily. 'Thought you'd promised Mum?' Val didn't bother to tell Ally the whole story. He was too tired and his head ached. He just fell into bed, dirty as he was. Len never even woke.

The next day, the whole of Magnolia Buildings was humming with gossip. Some people had seen the police car. Ginger's mother and father had had to go to the hospital. Ginger's arm had been set and he was now in plaster. Shorty, Thompson and George would be summoned. The rest of the gang had escaped, but the police were making inquiries.

To Val's relief, none of his gang blamed him for escaping, because they had all been too busy getting away themselves. George had lost yet another tooth in the fight.

'Have to get some dentures soon,' said Val, surveying his friend's wrecked mouth.

'My lip doesn't half hurt,' complained George. 'Still, we gave as good as we got. Nap's got a whopping black eye. I wish they'd send Shorty and Thompson to Borstal. Lucky I'm only eleven.'

'You'll get fined,' said Val, 'but not much. What's your Dad say?'

'Says he'll give me a leathering.' George grinned gap-toothedly. 'But he won't. He knows Shorty and Thompson.'

Mrs Doherty now collected an indignation meeting that moved from flat to flat. Sometimes Brian was taken along as the text of her sermon, to show what the gang had done to him: but the boy hated this and fled off to hide in the public library, where he could sit and read in peace. He was still at the Grammar School, but so good at his work that there were hopes of the University for him.

All the mothers agreed that Shorty's crowd were awful, and they all told Mrs Doherty that something should be done, and that they would speak to their husbands. The mothers of Val's gang joined up against the mothers of Shorty's gang; but the latter, who were as tough as their sons, knew more bad words and won these verbal fights. Sprot, the old caretaker, hearing the insults that were shouted from balcony to balcony, got in a panic and reported to his head office that real trouble was brewing.

The wives flew to their husbands, but they did not want to stir up trouble. They knew that they had to live next door to the other boys' fathers, to pass them frequently in the yard, and to meet them at the Cock or the Feathers. 'It's not my business,' was their sentiment. Only Ginger's father, who had red hair and a quick temper, made a fuss and wrote a letter to his Member of Parliament, saying that a question should be asked in the House about such gang fights.

Shorty, Thompson and George had to appear in the juvenile court, as they were the ones the police had managed to catch. But as it was their first official offence, they were only fined a few shillings and warned to be on good behaviour in the future. All three boys returned to the flats, jubilant at having got off so lightly. Then came the Whitsun holiday, and most people went off to the Dirt Track or the Dogs or to fish and picnic, and in the excitement of the holiday the row was forgotten.

So the two gangs were still left to fight out their own battle.

Chapter 13

SUMMER

IT was hot the day Mum came back from the convalescent home. A sudden early heat wave had put everyone into sun dresses, shot up the sale of iced lollies, filled the swimming pools, and brought all the trees rushing out into leaves and flowers. Mum still looked pale and shaky, but the flat was shining with cleanliness and everything had been tidied away.

'You've done grand,' cried Mum with some of her old liveliness, as she stood panting by the door, for four flights up had been a steep climb for her weak legs. 'Cor, why you've even got some flowers and the table all laid for tea!'

Ally felt a bit guilty, like a soldier who has put on a bit of spit and polish for the general's inspection, but who on ordinary days just slopped about. Still, she had done her best during these last days and she had provided proper meals.

Len came rushing in like a stone out of a catapult. He had run all the way home, because he had found a tiny, stray puppy, and must escape Mr Sprot if he were to get safely to the flat. He now put the puppy down and threw himself into Mum's arms, because, although he had forgotten temporarily about her return, he was glad indeed to see her.

'You been a good boy, Len?' asked Mum, kissing his crew cut which was the only bit of Len she could get at. 'Look, ducks, you can't keep a dog here.'

'Oh, Mum, I've got to. He's all by himself. He's lost.'

'But Mr Sprot will report it. You know that, Len. Cor, Ally, let's wet the tea.' And Mum sank down, looking suddenly exhausted.

'But, Mum,' argued Len. 'If we chuck the puppy out he'll die!'

'Shut up, Len!' cried Ally. 'Don't keep on keeping on.

Can't you see Mum's had it? There you are, Mum, good and strong and lots of sugar.'

Val rushed in looking quite as black as usual, but Mum was so thankful to see him that she made no remarks about his filthy face nor all the buttons missing. Doreen arrived with a pile of books, said 'Hullo, Mum,' as if her mother had just been

out for the day, and after eating a huge tea, went right on with homework as usual. Dad came back, and said, 'How are you, Marge? O.K.? That's right,' and went off to wash. But he looked very glad, for he hated the flat without Mum. It was so dull. Auntie Glad crept in later. Cold or hot weather, she wore her usual dark coat with her crocheted cap pulled over all her hair. She whispered something, sat down to her tea and said nothing as usual. But that didn't matter, because as soon as Mum had had two or three cups of tea, she was full of talk, all about the convalescent home, and what Sister had said, the food, and the ride back in the coach. Ally sat feeling relieved and happy. The responsibility of the family was now off her shoulders. They turned on the TV, and settled down to watch. It was the Bikini Girls dancing and all the Berners had glamour for half an hour.

'There's nothing like being home again,' said Mum as she sat beside Dad on the settee with Len wriggling near by.

Somehow, everyone had always felt Doreen would get her scholarship except Doreen herself. But then the news came that she had done so well in the papers that she was almost top of the list. Her essay had been adjudged a masterpiece of mature writing. Doreen was quite flummoxed. Long ago she had decided that essay was a terrible flop. Actually, she would never write anything so good or so heartfelt again, because it needed the pink pick-me-up to give her freedom to express her thoughts. But whether it was due to the pick-me-up or not, Doreen was now entitled to a place at the Green Coat School, one of the principal girls' schools of London. If Doreen worked hard, she would now certainly have a chance of going to the University.

'Yes, but what about clothes – and me out of work?' asked Mum.

'I've got to go to the Green Coats,' protested Doreen, very white-faced and tense. Surely her victory was not going to be snatched from her now and just for a few rags of garments? 'I must go now I've won it. I'll manage it. Can't we get the uniform secondhand or something?'

'Perhaps the Government'll help,' said Dad. 'They ought to, seeing the tax we pay on beer and tobacco. Cheer up, Dor. We'll get you the clothes, even if it means popping the family jewels.'

'That's right,' said Mum. 'We'll fix it somehow. Fancy me having a girl at the Green Coats! I must run along and tell Mrs Doherty and old nosey Crawley. This'll make them sit up. We didn't half hear about it when Brian got into the Grammar School. But this is the Green Coats! You've done very well, Dor!'

So it went on being a very hot summer. The flats were stifling, and the concrete yard outside smelt of hot dust. The foliage on the trees changed from small, yellow leaves into large dark green ones. The prams hardly stirred out of the shade. Once a week the band played on its stand, and sometimes there were concerts as well. The circus came as usual, and long queues stretched from the lighted big top right away into the darkness. Val and his gang of course managed to scrape together enough pennies to sit in the cheap seats, where they sat kicking the people on the plank below them. They yelled with joy all through the acts and felt they had never seen such clowns, such elephants, such tigers, although it was all exactly the same as last year. They went rushing home pretending to be ring masters, and for the next week played lassoing in the yard and were nearly scalped by old Sprot for tripping him up with their rope. Ally went to the circus with Lou and she sat and saw only glamour; glamour in the fine ladies who rode on elephants, glamour in the acrobats who threw each other about so negligently, glamour in the daredevils who rode bicycles high in the air. The music, the swooping, thumping band music, the lights and colours made her drunk with excitement. Len went on nagging and whining to see the circus, until Mum sent him off with Doreen; but he was so worried about the poor tigers who had to sit on chairs that he never slept all night. He hadn't thought the lions looked happy. 'Drat the circus,' said Mum in the small hours. 'This is the last time you go, Len Berners. Those tigers are all asleep now, curled up happy as a lot of cats. And you go to sleep too, or I'll give you such a slap.'

By July, all the talk was of holidays. Everybody everywhere asked everybody else, 'Where are you going for your holidays?' Some people had had theirs already and were going round looking like Red Indians with peeling noses, showing everyone their snapshots. Sticks of bright pink peppermint rock were being distributed to friends. Only the Berners family didn't talk about holidays, because they all knew they would not be able to go away that year. Money was short, and there would be extras to buy for Doreen.

'We'll go to Southend for the day when Dad gets his holiday,' said Mum consolingly.

It was almost the end of term and the class rooms were hot. Ally kept thinking of sandy coves where a cool sea ran up the beach. Oh, to be sunbathing! Even Miss Fleetwood reading the *Lotus Eaters* in her pretty voice did not raise Ally's spirits. Miss Fleetwood was going home to the Rectory and taking her young man. Lou was off to Margate, the Lotus Eaters had had a marvellous time. Only Ally Berners was going to be left in the hot, sticky town. It was not fair. She had worked so hard all the spring. She was tired. She ought to have a holiday. In a magazine story, a mysterious stranger would approach her and say, 'Are you Gloria Berners? The Rolls-Royce is waiting for you to take you to the yacht. Do not worry about clothes. We have a whole wardrobe of elegant garments packed and waiting on board.'

One day when she had climbed wearily up the stairs and gone along to the flat, she walked into such a tumult of people all yelling at her that she was absolutely bewildered. They were all shouting at once.

'Auntie Glad! Premium Bond. Holiday! Sea!'

'What?' Ally shouted back, transfixed in the doorway.

'Be quiet all of you,' cried Mum, her tired face now alive with excitement, her black eyes shining. 'Auntie Glad's won two hundred and fifty pounds with her Premium Bond . . .'

'She never!'

'And she's taking us all to the sea. She's booked a chalet and all for Dad's fortnight. Never told anyone. Just went and did it.'

Then all the family began to shout again, while Ally yelled back questions, and Auntie Glad sat there smiling a little, but quiet and withdrawn as usual.

'Eight pounds a week for those chalets.' Mum's voice rose

above the rest. 'But she says it's got a kitchen. And there's a shop and all, and a café too, right in the camp.'

After that, the whole world changed for the Berners children. They too could go round swanking about their holiday that was even more romantic than other people's because of the Premium Bond. Every day, when she woke up, Ally would yell out, 'Only ten days more, only eight, only five . . .' Until it was only one, and everything was packed and ready to start.

Chapter 14

THE HOLIDAY

IT wasn't a very long journey, and the railway station was not half a mile from the chalet camp, so they walked in procession along the sandy path that ran behind some dunes. Dad went first with the heaviest suitcase and the rest followed, each lugging a bundle. There had been no need to bring food as that could be bought at the camp shop.

'Cor, isn't it grand!' cried Mum, who was always enthusiastic, as she looked at the rather weather-worn little chalets that were dotted about the large field. They went straight to the office which was in a caravan, to fetch the key of their chalet, *Pebblecot*.

When they reached the chalet, there was tremendous excitement. The key of the door would not turn, because Mum shook so.

'Give it to me,' cried Dad. 'There! S'easy.' They all rushed in to look at the three bedrooms, the parlour with a divan, the kitchenette, the toilet, everybody talking and exclaiming at once. 'Can we sleep here, Mum?' 'What a small kitchen. It's worse than ours.' 'These beds are O.K.' 'Mind your great feet!' 'Mum, can I have a drink of water?' 'Mum, can we go to the beach?'

While all the rest of his family were surging round the chalet, Val did not stop a minute. He wasn't going to waste time on unpacking. All he wanted was to get to the sea, the sea he had not seen for three years. He ran across the field, dodging round the chalets and caravans through a hinterland of brambles, and came to the edge of a low cliff. And there was the sea!

No sailor cooped up for years in a dark prison could have eyed the ocean with more delight. Although Val did not put his feeling into any sort of words, he knew that it was what he wanted . . . water, light, air, and space. He stood for a second breathing in the salt wind, and then he began to run down the rough track to the shore.

The coastline here was a long, low line of cliffs that fell to sandy beaches. There were no magnificent views, just miles and miles of sand, and a shallow sea that ebbed away out of view twice a day, leaving great wet lagoons that the waves refilled on each visit. On this particular evening, the sky was pinkish and all these lagoons were pink too. Val threw off his shoes and socks, not worrying where they fell, and ran on, feeling the joy of wet sand under his toes. His only idea was to get to the water. He was like an explorer, heading for the unknown, into the sunset, into space. He was a boat, a plane, a space ship, anything that travelled fast. There were no more streets, no more Shorty, no more cops or school. The only thing in the world was that line of pale, opal water far, far ahead. Val splashed through the lagoons, and the water was tepid. He left his footprints over acres of virgin sand, he leapt tide lines of shells, corks, and feathers, and then crossed a last, higher cheek of sand and came to the quiet sea that scarcely seemed to move. He was into it, calf deep, knee deep, thigh deep with no thought of his carelessly rolled up clothes, nor of his new shoes left unguarded. He dabbled his fingers in the water and licked them to taste the salt. He wished he had his costume but it was too much trouble to go back for it. The sea was all around him and everything was quiet. He was quite alone, but not at all frightened. To be alone in such a great expanse of water was a treat and a rest. He just stood there for a long time, feeling the last rays of sun on his head, and he licked his salty lips. He was in the sea at last!

When he came out, he felt hungry and went back to look for his shoes. It took some time to find them, and he was afraid they had been stolen, but at last he saw them amongst the pebbles. With his wet trousers clinging to his legs, he started back up the path. At the top, he met a fat, smiling little man.

'Had a good paddle, son?' asked the man beaming all over his face. Val thought him quite old. He must have been about forty. Extreme good nature and kindness oozed out of him. He was obviously such a friendly person that he was hardly safe to be loose in a wicked world.

'Smashing,' said Val.

'It's a nice place,' said the fat little man. 'You got a chalet?'

'That's right.' Val did not wish to stay and talk, as his whole mind was full of tea. 'Number fifteen we've got. Just come today.'

'There, isn't that a coincidence?' The little man beamed all over his chubby face. 'Me and my sister's got fourteen. Our name is Truby. Are you a big family?'

Val had learnt not to give his name to strangers, but he answered, 'Seven, if you count Mum and Dad and Auntie Glad.'

'And how will you all fit into the chalet?' asked the little man with friendly curiosity.

'Dunno,' said Val. 'Haven't been inside yet.'

As they walked towards the chalet, they saw that all the Berners family was busy moving in. Mum had opened the windows, Dad had got out two deckchairs that were meant for the small porch. Doreen was running back from the camp shop with a basket of food. As they came nearer, Val could hear Mum's excited voice. 'Put it there! Clumsy! Move yourself. Ally, pass me that.' Inside the house, Ally was singing at the top of her voice: 'I love you Mondays, Tuesdays, Wednesdays . . .' Len rushed out yelling, 'I want to go to the beach.'

'What a jolly family!' sighed Mr Truby sentimentally. 'I am glad you are next door to us.' He might have said more, if a furious, raucous voice had not shouted, 'Willyum! Come in at once. Your tea's been ready for half an hour.' A thin, elderly woman came bouncing out of number fourteen. She had a face like a lemon, and was obviously in a furious temper.

'Oh, dear,' exclaimed little Mr Truby. 'I must run!' And he did hurry across the grass as fast as he could on his short

legs. The moment he got near the house, his sister popped out again and began to screech, 'Where've you been? My head's awful. Those terrible people who've just moved in, kicking up such a shindy. I'll complain to the – ' and she banged the door behind her brother.

The Berners had a splendid meal of sausages and chips, bread and jam and plenty of hot, strong tea. Everybody was already full of news and discoveries.

'There's pictures on Thursday evenings up at the café,' Doreen said. 'And a festival in town on Friday night. And, Mum, could I buy a bathing cap? They've got lovely ones at the shop.'

Ally said, 'I met ever such a nice girl, Mum. She's called Audrey. She says her Mum says I can go and look at their chalet. Audrey's got a proper playsuit and all.'

A man had told Dad that the nearest pub was the Ring of

Bells, a snug little place a quarter of a mile up the road. He and Dad had made a date for six-thirty. The camp was playing a darts match there on Saturday.

The family soon settled in to enjoy itself. The weather was fine and warm, and the children spent nearly all day in the sea, while Mum sat thankfully on the sand and kept her weight off her feet, and gave out buns and sandwiches and sweets and drinks as frequently as if she were a one woman snack bar. All the family became a fiery red, and poor Doreen, who had a fair skin, was in such agonies from sunburn that she could not sleep at night, though Mum plastered her with calamine. However, in a few days, the tender skin peeled off and everyone attained a nice shade of brown. Dad lay in the sun and went to sleep beneath his paper, and in the evenings joined the other men at the Ring of Bells. Len changed out of all recognition after a few days' sun and air. He ate enormous meals and stopped worrying about stray dogs or poor crabs with no homes to go to.

But the person who changed most was Auntie Glad. The first morning, she made the family gasp, for she came to breakfast in a new, blue striped cotton frock, and her head tied up in a scarf to match. For the first time in years, the family really looked at her. In the flat, wearing her dark coat and her crocheted cap pulled down to her ears, she had been so invisible as to be nearly transparent.

'Cor, Glad!' cried Mum, quite taken aback. 'Why, you look smashing. Where did you get that frock? It doesn't half show up your eyes.'

The family gaped, and realized for the first time that Auntie Glad's eyes were blue.

'Thought you were putting your bit of money in the post office,' said Dad, who although glad to have a holiday, felt disquiet that Auntie Glad should bust her whole windfall.

'I'm tired of putting my money in the post office,' Auntie Glad suddenly said in quite a loud, clear voice. 'I've been doing it all my life. Now I'm going to spend a bit.'

'Cor, Glad!' said Mum. 'You are going it!'

As the days went by, although Auntie Glad did not speak much more than usual, she did become increasingly visible. The greyness went out of her tired face, the colour came back into her eyes and cheeks, and now that she had taken off the black cap, her hair got loose in the wind and took some colour from the sun. It seemed to have quite a golden glow, whereas before it had been a drab mouse shade. She was not, however, any more sociable than usual, but would take a rug and a magazine and go off by herself to the dunes or the cliffs. Some days she took a sandwich and did not even return to dinner. She seemed glad to be alone and out of doors.

Instead of always being black, Val was now always soaking wet. He seldom wore more than bathing shorts. Ally had struck up a friendship with Audrey, and was quite engrossed by Audrey's family who lived at Purley and were very grand and glamorous.

'Mum, Audrey goes to a private school, and her Mum thinks my hair's lovely. They're going to ask me to Purley when we get back.'

It was all Audrey, Audrey, till Mum said she'd scream out loud if she heard the name again.

Ally and Audrey walked about arm in arm all day and bathed together, or spent hours drinking soft drinks up at the camp café.

If the boys tried to talk to them, they giggled and turned their backs. They did not want to waste their precious time together with stupid boys. 'They're so silly, Mum,' said Ally. 'Why can't they act more like the chaps in pictures?'

One evening, Val was messing about on the beach, when Mr Truby came up. 'Hullo, Val! Enjoying yourself?' The little man always tried to be friendly when his sister was not about. The Berners could sometimes hear Miss Truby yelling at her brother right across in their chalet.

'Yes,' said Val, who could not imagine that any boy could be unhappy by the sea. The only horror was the thought of having to go back to London, and the days were now slipping away fast.

'Don't want to go home, eh?' said Mr Truby, sitting down slowly on the pebbles.

'No,' said Val. 'I hate it at home. I'd like to live here.'

'Why don't you like it?'

'Don't know. Nothing to do and too many people.' Val chucked a stone at a gull. 'I hate school too. The masters are wet.'

'I don't want to go back either,' said Mr Truby with a sigh. 'I'm a sanitary engineer. Doing quite well, but I like the country. But Aggie, my sister, she hates it.'

'You can't get out of London. It's too big, see.' Val was considering the matter. 'Now if I had a bike, I'd get out every week . . .'

'Get a job evenings and earn one,' suggested the little man. 'You're a big strong boy.'

'Earn one,' Val said bitterly. 'I can't get a job anywhere. I tried all round the Common. I'll never get a bike.' He sighed now, thinking of that forlorn hope for freedom.

'I've got an old bike,' said Mr Truby suddenly. 'Don't see why you shouldn't have it . . .'

'You mean?' Val stared at him as though a bicycle had just floated down from the skies. 'Cor, Mister, I'd try and save up and pay you bit by bit. It might take time.'

'Bless the boy.' Mr Truby beamed. 'I'd give it you. I never use it. Haven't got the wind these days for pedalling uphill. You come along and fetch it. I live down Wandsworth way. But come when my sister isn't there. She's not one for giving things away.'

'Cor! A bike of my own.' Val's voice was rapt. 'Can I come as soon as we go back?'

The holiday was over, and on the last evening, Mum was packing, helped by Ally. All the family were sad at leaving *Pebblecot*, and only Val was buoyed up with the thought of the bike.

The chalet was in chaos, everyone running round in circles, trying to make dirty clothes fit into cases that had comfortably held clean ones. Even Dad was being made to help. 'You fasten it while I kneel on it,' Mum was crying. 'Cor, if that hasp hasn't bust. Got a bit of cord?' Mum after two weeks of sun and air was quite herself again, laughing, talking, and friends with the whole camp. All the evening innumerable ladies had dropped in to wish her farewell.

Auntie Glad was not packing. She was not in the chalet at all. Once she had paid the two weeks' rent, she had taken no more responsibility for the chores than she did at home. She was always out of doors by herself.

'Put your finger there,' said Dad to Mum, as he tied the cord round the case. At that moment Auntie Glad came slipping through the outer door and behind her was Mr Truby.

'Hullo,' said Auntie Glad in her soft voice. 'Here's Mr Truby.' But there was something about the pair of them that made everyone pause and stare. They had not just come in together, they were somehow a couple.

'Marge,' said Auntie Glad. 'Me and Mr Truby are getting married.'

'What?' cried everybody.

'Glad! You're never?' Mum struggled up from the floor. 'Why, I didn't even know you knew him.'

Mr Truby, who had been looking rather shy, exchanged a laughing glance with Auntie Glad, who for the first time the Berners family remembered, suddenly laughed out loud.

'Course I know her,' said Mr Truby. 'Seeing as we've spent every day of this fortnight together, haven't we, Glad?'

Auntie Glad had become completely visible. She was smiling, she had colour, and she wore a pink dress that the family had never seen before. Her eyes were a periwinkle blue. She had come alive. She and Mr Truby made the smallest pair imaginable, for he was scarcely taller than she was. But they were both so happy it was a joy to see them. There's glamour about them, thought Ally, and this seemed very odd to her.

'The only thing is,' said Mr Truby, 'don't tell my sister.'

'She'll have to know sooner or later, won't she?' asked Dad.

Mr Truby looked frightened. 'I'd rather wait till we get home. I don't want her kicking up down here, and she will kick up.' His merry little face grew quite grave. 'Still, she's got money. She can have a place of her own. She won't need to live with us.'

'That's right,' said Mum. 'You start as you mean to go on. And it'll be nice for Glad to have a place of her own. What with always living with Grandma and then with us. I hope you'll be very happy. My, Glad, aren't you a sly one!' And she kissed her tiny sister-in-law, who looked sly all of a sudden.

Then everyone burst out laughing. Dad dug out a private supply of beer, the children were sent for fish and chips, and the whole party settled down to a wonderful evening, with Mr Truby and Auntie Glad telling all their adventures in chorus. How they first met up at the ice cream kiosk, how they went to the pictures, how they escaped from his sister, Aggie, the saga of the whole fortnight.

'Well, here's to your jolly good health and may all your troubles be little ones,' cried Dad, raising his glass. The children started to sing 'For they are jolly good fellows,' and then came a loud rap on the door.

Ally flew to open it. 'Must be Audrey,' she said. But it wasn't. It was Miss Truby in a forbidding grey mackintosh. She looked furious and her mouth was pursed. 'Excuse me. Is my brother here?'

Before Ally could answer, or stop her, Miss Truby went marching into the room, and must have seen all the signs of jollification.

'So there you are!' she shouted. 'Sneaking off and leaving me alone day and night in this God-forsaken place. I know what you've been up to. I saw you and her' (pointing at Auntie Glad) 'sneaking round by the huts. I've been watching you all this week, William Truby. You nasty, sneaking little man!'

Mr Truby stood up. He was much shorter than his sister.

'I – I was going to tell you, Aggie,' he stammered. 'I'm engaged to be married to Miss Berners.'

'What, her?' said Miss Truby, throwing a ton of scorn into her voice.

'And why not?' asked Mum whose black eyes shone dangerously. 'If you can't be pleasant, perhaps you'd go home.'

'I will not. William, you've been entrapped by a wicked, scheming baggage . . .'

But this was too much for Mum, who shot round the table and confronted Miss Truby. 'Glad's not wicked nor scheming,' she cried. 'She's as decent and kind and hard-working a person as your brother'll ever find, and she paid for us all to come here and have a holiday out of her own pocket. Your brother's a lucky man.'

'Hear, hear,' said Dad, banging his fist on the table.

'And if you can behave decently,' went on Mum, 'and sit down quietly like a lady, I'll get you a cup of tea and we'll talk this over sensibly.'

But Miss Truby's stern face suddenly seemed to be breaking up, as if an earthquake were taking place beneath it. She sank into a chair and started to sob and gulp. For the next few minutes she had hysterics. Mum flew to put on a kettle. Dad edged towards the door. Len began to whimper. Ally and Doreen gaped. Mr Truby was obviously very frightened. He had always been defeated by his kind heart, and when his sister had hysterics he got into a terrible state. Now he kept patting her on the shoulder. She clutched at him: 'Oh, Willy, what should I do without you? You can't go off with that woman.'

'Well, we'll see, we'll see. We shan't be getting married just yet, Aggie. So don't worry. There, there.'

But Auntie Glad, who had not spoken a word during this whole scene, now saw the danger light. She had suddenly guessed what always happened to Mr Truby each time he tried to get married. She stood up, and cried out, 'That's not true, Bill. You and me are getting married at once, next month,

or not at all. Otherwise we'll never get married. She'll talk you out of it like she did last time.'

'Last time?' said Mr Truby, getting very red. 'How did you know about last time?'

'Got some sense, haven't I?' asked Auntie Glad. She stood up very erect, all of her five feet, and she was so roused and angry that her family hardly knew her. 'A man like you, Bill, would have married years ago if it hadn't been for her.' She pointed at Aggie who was moaning in her chair. 'But if you let me down, Bill, I'll sue you for breach of promise, and that's that.'

Poor William really did look like a man between two fires. He had no idea that Glad could have such sharp teeth. At the end of her speech, Auntie Glad sat down with a thump as if she had astonished herself. But although she did not speak again, her face was determined.

In the end, William took the sobbing Aggie off. She was still sniffing and clinging to her brother.

'Cor, Glad!' said Mum, who still held a full teapot in mid-air. 'You could have knocked me down with a feather. I never heard you speak up like that before.'

'She's a wicked woman,' said Auntie Glad, and her voice

was no longer its old shy whisper. 'If I don't rescue him now, Marge, he'll never get away.'

'That's right,' said Dad. 'If you want a man, Glad, go and get him. Well, if you girls can hold the fort for a bit, I'm going up to the Bells for my half pint. I need it after that little do.'

Ally went to bed full of excitement. This was real drama. No heroine on the pictures could have spoken up better than quiet little Auntie Glad. If that was what love did to you – gosh!

Val also went to bed happy. Mr Truby must give him the bike now. Why, the man would be a relation! An uncle!

'The best of it is,' said Doreen to Ally as they undressed, 'when Auntie Glad marries, we can each have a bed to ourselves, and I shan't have you doing your beastly exercises all over me.'

'Fancy Glad!' said Mum as she rolled into bed. 'Remind me to stop the milk tomorrow.'

Chapter 15

'SOMETHING ABOUT GUNS'

NOW it was autumn on the Common. The chestnut leaves that had been the first to unfurl were turning yellow and orange, and loosening their hold upon the twigs. Soon they would come drifting down, and there would be a smell of bonfires rising from all the gardens. A few games of cricket survived like last roses of summer, but the footballers had really invaded the fields. The prams were moving more briskly now, and it was only on specially hot days that the old men got out their draughts and dominoes. Later came the early morning frosts, and people everywhere began to shake the mothballs out of their winter clothes.

The Berners children never played with each other. They all lived such different and separate lives that they usually met only for meals and then parted again. Yet, while September moved towards October, Ally did notice that something was wrong with Val. It may have been because she was growing up, but she had suddenly become more conscious of other people and their feelings. Until now, other people had just been part of the scenery of a world where she walked in a dream. Yes, in spite of the new bicycle, Val did seem worried. He walked about with a furtive air, as though he were afraid of something.

Looks as if a bogy might jump out at him any minute, thought Ally. Wonder what he's been up to? But she did not dare ask him as she knew he would only tell her to shut up.

Actually it was George who had disturbed Val's peace of mind. The two boys had gone off to Hampton Court one sunny afternoon. It was Val's first long ride on his bike, and the whole expedition to him seemed magical. Instead of being cooped up in the yard and the streets around the Common, here he was sailing along between the cars and buses, able to visit really remote places like Hampton Court.

The boys went straight to the Maze. They knew all about it from reading *Three Men in a Boat* at school. As soon as they had paid their pennies, and were let into the labyrinth, they started to run madly along the paths between the high green hedges, and as they ran, they kept bumping into other children who were running back from dead ends. Val and George ran and ran, shouting all the way. They kept taking turns that brought them to full stops against green hedges, and it was a long time before they reached the two trees in the middle, and longer still before they got back to the turnstile. They both were certain they knew the right way. 'Go on! It's here.' 'No, you ass, it's this way. Get out. I've seen that bit of paper before!' Everybody else was laughing and running and shouting. It was the greatest fun.

After they had done the Maze, the boys wandered down by the water to look for conkers and to admire the ducks who kept standing on their heads.

While Val chucked twigs and small stones at the ducks, George said suddenly, 'Shorty's lot are up to something.'

Ever since the holidays, the gang had been rather quiet. Val had hoped they had given up persecuting him and had found themselves girl friends.

'Thought Shorty'd got a girl,' he said. 'That Pam Stringer?'

'No. 'Tisn't girls,' said George looking worried. ' 'S'matter of fact, I heard something last week. Nap and Shorty were talking, see, on our balcony.' George had the misfortune to inhabit the same balcony as Nap. 'They were saying something about guns. You know the way Nap laughs, and then he said, "Don't you worry, Shorty, I'll get those guns. There's always the roof".'

'What guns?' asked Val.

'Dunno. Didn't dare stay. They might have copped me listening.' George ruffled his two-coloured crop, and stuck his tongue in between his gappy teeth as he always did when thinking of the gang.

'Cor,' said Val, thoughtfully, 'if that lot got guns, it'd be awful. Where'd they get them from?'

'Dunno. But they're up to something. Why've they been letting us alone? Young Bill cheeked them last week and they didn't bother to chase him up. It's kind of queer, Val.'

For the next few days Val and George tried to find out what Shorty's lot were doing, but they did not tell the rest of their friends about this investigation. Billy was a big mouth and Brian did not seem interested these days.

Although Val did not find out much, he became sure that some scheme was afoot. He was quite haunted by the idea that Shorty and his crowd might soon be armed. If they got guns Magnolia Buildings would be untenable. He did not reflect that firearms would soon be discovered and taken away. He had a vivid mental picture of Shorty and Nap shooting up everyone, barricading the stairs and balconies. Val had seen a boy like that on the pictures. He had shot up a whole school, and taken a child as hostage.

Then Ally became involved. Since the summer, she had changed a lot. She was suddenly growing up and getting slimmer, because now she was almost fifteen. Overnight, as it seemed, she was getting quite clean and tidy. She no longer made spasmodic attempts at glamour, but brushed her hair and teeth every day, and even polished her shoes. Her stocking seams went straight down the backs of her legs, and her clothes looked well ironed. She was really very pretty, and she longed for new clothes more than anything on earth. Yet, how could she have new clothes, for she was not earning money, and every spare penny of the family cash had had to be spent on Doreen who was now at the Green Coats School? Ally, like everyone else in the Buildings, wanted to make money, but how? She decided to go and discuss the matter with Lou, and was on her way there one evening when she ran into Shorty.

Six months ago, Shorty would have barged into her on the stairs, pulled her pony tail, or made a rude noise, but now he stood aside to let her pass. Ally did not want to stop and talk because she had never liked him. His head was too big for his body, and he had short legs. She also disliked his unhealthy pasty face, and his green eyes. When he asked, 'Where are you off to, Ally?' she answered, 'To see a friend,' and slipped quickly past him and away down the stairs.

After that, Shorty always seemed to be decorating her balcony, or hanging about the stairs saying stupid things that had no obvious meaning, until Ally was quite nervous about leaving the flat.

This had been going on for about a fortnight, when one evening she was coming home up the stairs and by chance Val was a flight behind her. Shorty was at the top of her landing, and he gave one of his nastier whistles on seeing her. He had reached the point now when he tried to irritate Ally, as that was the only way to get her attention. Ally pretended not to see him, but Shorty caught at her wrist. 'What you being so toffy-nosed for?'

'You leave me alone,' cried Ally angrily and twisted her wrist free.

Shorty laughed, but she knew he was angry because she did not like him. Val, coming up the steps from below, saw this scene, and realized with horror that he ought to rescue Ally. But for all his short legs, Shorty had strong arms and shoulders, and he could punch like a steam-hammer if he were roused. Before Val could close in for an attack, Brian Doherty appeared above and said to Shorty, 'Leave her alone, or I'll make you.' Ally dodged round Brian and out of the way.

'So she's your girl now, is she?' said Shorty unpleasantly. Brian had grown so much he overtopped Shorty by about six inches. He looked quite prepared to fight, although he was thin and willowy and might not have stood up to Shorty for long.

'You get out of here,' shouted Brian, 'and don't be making a nuisance of yourself.'

There was a pause while the two boys squared up to each other.

'You – !' said Brian, waiting to spring. Val came running up, and when Shorty saw he was outnumbered, he gave a forced laugh. 'Really, I can't be bothered with you kids,' he said and brushed past Val down the stairs. Val was so surprised that he let him go.

'Been getting fresh, has he?' Brian was saying to Ally.

Ally tossed her mane of curls. 'He's always hanging around. I told him where he got off.'

'You leave him to me,' said Brian. Ally looked at her champion with sudden admiration.

Soppy, thought Val and went along to 49. But later that evening, he said to Ally, 'You know that Shorty. He's up to something.'

'You're telling me,' said Ally. 'Pity there's no more call-up for his lot. Army'd do him good. I wish he was out of this place.'

'Oh, I don't mean girls and that,' said Val. 'But George says . . .' He looked round nervously. 'You won't say anything, Ally. George thinks him and Nap are getting some guns.'

Ally laughed. 'Where'd they get guns from? Don't be daft, Val. I know I'd like to take a gun to him. The sauce!'

Chapter 16

THE WEDDING

AUNTIE GLAD'S wedding was the first week in October. She had got her way and had stuck to her ultimatum. Either William married her at once or not at all.

'Glad's a sticker,' William told Dad while they were having a quick one at the Cock, for the two men had become great friends. 'And her such a little bit of a thing. You wouldn't credit it to look at her. Well, it's all fixed, and I've got myself a new suit.'

Somehow, Auntie Glad had sister Aggie out of William's house and into a flat all in six weeks. For it turned out that William was quite well off and had a nice little business of his own as a sanitary engineer. He kept an office, a van and a couple of men, and all the housewives loved him because he was so sympathetic about their plumbing troubles.

'Auntie Glad, you'll be quite rich and grand!' exclaimed Ally when they stood outside the semi-detached villa in Crill-stead Road. She and Mum had gone over with Auntie Glad to inspect the house as soon as Aggie was safely away.

The house was furnished with solid mahogany pieces, and the windows were so shrouded in heavy lace curtains that the light of day scarcely penetrated. Aggie had taken away a lot of ornaments to her flat, but there were still enough objects on crocheted mats to make Mum cry, 'What a place! Think of the dusting.' She poked round a bit and tried all the chairs. 'Still this is a nice suite, Glad. If you paper up the walls, and do over this brown paint and hang some fresh curtains, it'll be O.K. Come on upstairs and let's have a look, ducks.'

All the furniture upstairs was just as huge and solid, and filled each room so that it was hard to dodge round it. Mum bounced on the beds. 'You'll need new mattresses, Glad. This one's stuffed with old road blocks.' And Mum gave one of her hearty laughs. 'And I've never seen such thick lace curtains. They shut out all the light. Still, I must say the bathroom's ever so nice.'

Glad said nothing much, as usual, and just went round quietly opening all the drawers and cupboards, but Ally guessed that she had plenty of ideas, and that Uncle William would have to agree with them.

Auntie Glad had insisted on a white wedding, with bridesmaids and all the trimmings. 'I've got the money,' she said, 'and seeing as I never thought I'd get married, I'm going to have the lot! After all, Marge, it's only once in a lifetime, and William's quite agreeable.'

Uncle William had just said amiably that he didn't mind being a circus.

Ally and Doreen were to be bridesmaids. A grand wedding breakfast was to be held in the big room over the Cock. Dad fixed that. Being a regular customer, he had influence. Dad also fixed the bell-ringers to give Auntie Glad a nice peal, for he knew them all, as they came over to the Cock to be refreshed after practising. Auntie Glad was to be married at the Church on the Common, which was only five hundred yards from Magnolia Buildings. She and her retinue could easily have walked across, but Uncle William insisted that the whole thing should be done properly. So the two Rolls Royces that went to every wedding and funeral on the Common, were ordered, and decked with white streamers.

Words cannot describe the excitement and commotion in 49 on the morning of the wedding.

Auntie Glad had copied her dress from a Hartnell one that had been in the workroom, and it was a miracle of loveliness, a pale satin that had a silver sheen. Mrs Doherty, Mrs Crawley and various other Magnolia ladies had been in to see it where it lay on Mum's bed. Ally and Doreen were to wear dresses of coral velvet, with wreaths of flowers like small coronets, and pink velvet shoes. Mum had bought a new hat. 'That's all I can afford,' she explained. 'Still, my maroon coat's quite good, and I'd have had to have a new felt in any case.' Dad and the boys were to wear their Sunday suits. When the bouquets were sent from the shop, the family found that Uncle William had ordered enormous buttonholes too.

'I'll look like a flower show,' said Dad as he was handed his.

The question was who was to dress first and where. Ally and Doreen would obviously need a lot of titivating, but if the boys were got ready too soon, they would be filthy before they reached the church. Mum rushed round, tying ties, and doing hair, and she finally got the boys into their tidy suits, pinned on their buttonholes, and practically tethered them to two chairs with such awful threats of no party and no cake that even Val did not dare to move.

Auntie Glad dressed in Mum's room, and the girls were still having their wreaths adjusted when the Rolls were reported to be at the door.

Everyone who was at home, and most people were as it was a Saturday afternoon, stood at their doors, or leant over their balconies.

'This is glamour, real glamour at last,' thought Ally to herself, for she had seen her own reflection in the mirror and knew that she was looking beautiful. Holding her bouquet of pink roses and chrysanthemums, she went carefully down the stairs with Doreen following her. This is the way I shall walk when I'm a bride, she thought.

'There's lovely, she is,' cried Mrs Doherty as they passed her door. 'You'll be the next, Ally!'

'Your petticoat's showing a mite.' Mrs Crawley could never bear to admire without adding adverse criticism. 'Still, even that Doreen is looking all right today,' she said audibly to Mrs Doherty.

Doreen followed along stolidly. She did not care. She took less interest in her velvet frock than in her green school coat, for that garment was the emblem of her career and success.

Down the stairs went Ally, and at each balcony, there were

admiring 'ohs' and 'ahs'. Just for one day she was not ordinary Ally Berners but some wonderful creature who was touched by romance. Shorty and Nap in their Italian suits were hanging about as usual, but today they dared not speak to her or even whistle rudely, for they were quite awed.

In the concrete yard the Rolls were standing, and there were chauffeurs in uniform to open the door, and to hand in Ally. This was their second trip to the church, for Mum, hot and flustered in her maroon coat, had gone off with the boys. Grandpa and Grandma had also gone in the first trip. They had come up to London for the day, bringing a basket of fruit and flowers. Only Auntie Glad, sitting serene and quiet in her silver dress, still remained upstairs with Dad, who was to give her away.

Ally got into the Rolls like a princess, and felt a bit annoyed at having to share this joy with Doreen who just flumped down beside her. In Ally's ears was music, the swelling, angel voices that always accompany heroines of the pictures during their great moments.

'Hold your bouquet up, you clot,' she whispered to Doreen. 'You're getting it all banged about.' There was a sort of cheer from the children as the Rolls drove off. Some ran a little way after it, to watch it up the road. Ally held her bouquet high and looked out of the window. She saw all the people watching her, and she could hardly breathe for excitement. She wished this drive could last for hours and hours.

When the Rolls drew up in front of the church, there was quite a little crowd of bystanders, all the people who came to gape at the Saturday weddings. The photographer was there too, unfurling his equipment. The chauffeur handed Doreen out of the car, but her wreath was already a little crooked on her straight, red hair. Ally got out as gracefully as possible.

She and Doreen stood in the porch waiting for the Rolls to bring Auntie Glad. When Ally saw it drive up, her heart missed a beat. Dad got out first to help Antie Glad. Even through the veil, Ally could see how calm and happy the little woman looked. Dad with his huge buttonhole, looked as miserable as any man could, and he was only buoying himself up with the hope of soon being back at the familiar Cock.

Somehow the procession formed up. Auntie Glad took Dad's arm. A woman in the porch straightened Doreen's wreath, and the two girls fell in behind. They were all walking up to the altar, to the waiting Rector, and to Uncle William who was standing there with his hands clasped tightly behind his back.

This is love, thought Ally, as the Rector read the reasons for which marriage is ordained. This is what Izzy Waters is singing about. Perhaps this is why Shorty is always hanging around. This is why Mum and Dad have stayed together. How beautiful it is! One day it will happen to me. I shall stand here by a man, and I shall turn to look at that man as Auntie Glad is looking at Uncle William. Now he is putting on the ring. One day, I shall have a ring too.

Then the bridal party moved into the vestry and everyone started kissing everyone else. At last they were all out on the pillared portico, and the photographer was arranging them in the October sunshine, and imploring them to smile. First he took Auntie Glad, who now had her veil thrown back. Uncle William was holding her hand and beaming all over his face. Then the photographer took the bride and groom with the bridesmaids and their families. The last group included everyone, even Aggie, who had sniffed into a lace-edged hanky right through the service.

The Rolls Royces drew alongside and drove the party across to the Cock, where the wedding feast was served in the upper room. They had cold roast chicken with salad, trifles, fruit salad, with a sweet wine in which to toast the happy pair.

This is the wedding breakfast, Ally told herself, looking down the table. Tomorrow it will all be finished and I've got to remember it always. Auntie Glad is going to cut the cake. Val, the pig, has got his plate up already. H'm, Dad looks a bit more cheerful now. Doreen's upset the trifle all down her frock. She would! Look at Mum laughing! She doesn't half get red in the face. 'Good health to the happy pair!' Gosh, wine does taste queer, not at all like grapes. Now that silly best man, with his stupid jokes, is going to read the telegrams. Poor Dad. He doesn't want to make his speech. Come on, Dad!

After the breakfast, more friends came in, and there were sausage rolls and cake and lots of drinks. The record player was turned on and everybody danced. Auntie Glad was led off first by her William. The Dohertys had come, and the Crawleys and some of the girls from the workroom, a few of Uncle William's pals, and a chum or two of Dad's who had wandered up from below. Grandma and Grandpa sat side by side, holding their glasses of port, and nodding their heads to the tunes while everyone else jogged by. Ally went bumping round with Brian, for neither of them were expert dancers. The boys tore about getting under everybody's feet and Mum had to rush Doreen to the cloakroom as she was sick. Mr Porlock, the Cock's host, had come up to drink a health to the bride and groom, and he was making Mum scarlet with laughter with his jokes. But Mum refused to dance with him. 'On my feet enough without that,' she said. 'Get along with you, Mr Porlock. You ask one of the girls.'

The party went on and on, the music blared and jigged. Everyone got very hot and cheerful, and forgot all about their solemn thoughts in church. It was almost time for Auntie Glad to go and change her frock and to start off home with Uncle William. They were not having a honeymoon, both having already taken a holiday that year. At this very moment, the barman came hurrying in, and whispered something to Mr Porlock. The word he whispered was 'police'.

'Police?' asked Mr Porlock, looking hurriedly at his watch. 'It's not closing time yet?'

'Well,' said the barman. 'There's been a robbery next door. The police want to know where the owner of the shop lives.'

'Excuse me, all,' said Mr Porlock, and he went quickly out of the room. Some of Dad's friends and Dad went after him.

Dad had been longing to get down to his usual corner in the bar and this was a good chance. Auntie Glad had gone off to change, and Mum began to collect up the children. Val, however, slid away, and went downstairs behind the men.

There were two policemen in the bar, and they were soon writing down the address of the shop's owner in their note-books.

'Lives just round the corner, he does,' said Mr Porlock. 'I don't know the number, see, but it's the second house in Crawford Terrace. What's happened, Sergeant?'

'Lady across the road phoned the station. Said she saw two boys on the roof and thought something must be wrong as she knew the shop was shut.'

The police, Mr Porlock and most of the customers went out of the bar and into the small alley that ran up between the Cock and the shops. These shops were the kind that are built in front of ordinary houses. They were just one storey high, and were lit at the back by a large, glass skylight. The burgled shop sold junk: chipped china, old guitars, mattresses, books, beds, toys, and cheap lines of every kind. In the narrow alley there was a ladder propped against the house wall.

'That's my ladder!' cried Mr Porlock. 'It was in my yard. How did they get it out of there?'

'Those boys climb like monkeys,' said the Sergeant. 'Bates you'd better go down and fetch the owner.' The constable went off while the sergeant and Mr Porlock went up on the roof to have another look at the forced skylight. In the darkness, Val went up the ladder too, but was sternly sent down again. So he wandered round the front of the shop and had a look into the window there. Already a suspicion was forming in his mind. By the light of the street lamps, he peered in at the queer assortment of objects for sale. There were old radios, shoes tied up in pairs, gas stoves, but not the object for which Val searched. He was almost certain that during the last week he had noticed a rifle in the window. Now it wasn't there. Overhead, the men were still talking and walking about, examining the roof for clues.

Roof, gun. The words reminded Val of the words that George had overheard spoken by Nap. It must have been Shorty's lot who had broken into the shop. They had known somehow about the ladder at the Cock – of course, Nap's mum cleaned there. They had got on to the roof and would never have been seen except for the chance of this woman looking out of her bedroom window and catching their silhouettes against the night sky.

What'll I do? thought Val. He had started instinctively to run along the pavement, to shout out his discovery to the police, but then he checked his feet. Much as he disliked Shorty and Co., he did not care to turn informer. He did not want to hand anyone over to the cops. Besides, if the boys knew he had sneaked, they would half kill him. Gosh, what was he to do?

He stood there on the pavement, trying to decide. He was so tempted. If Shorty's lot were sent to Borstal, the Buildings would be a far happier place. Val longed to have George to discuss the problem with.

Mr Crabbe, the shop owner, had arrived by now, and was unlocking the shop door and talking to the police and Mr Porlock. The rest of the men had wandered back to their drinks in the bar. Val waited, still watching, while Mr Crabbe switched on the lights and began to look round the shop to see what was missing. Val held his breath when the men approached the window, and he saw Mr Crabbe pointing out the spot where the rifle had been. Val knew that he was right. The rifle *had* been stolen. In his own mind, he saw Shorty and Co. running across the dark grass of the Common, with the gun hidden beneath their coats. They would be in bed by now with the gun tucked under a mattress.

The police, having written everything down in their notebooks, were now leaving the shop. The sergeant was saying: 'We'll see what we can do about this, sir. Sure nothing else is missing?'

Mr Crabbe shook his head. 'No, sergeant, just that rifle and the revolver.'

'Till not touched? Nothing in it, eh? Still, that woman was right. It's probably boys. A man would have gone for the cash. And I've got some suspicions about the gang that did it.' He turned to the constable. 'Bates. Help Mr Porlock shift his ladder. Better not leave it there.' Then he noticed Val. 'Here, you, what are you doing, still hanging about? You ought to be in bed, son.' For Val had by now transferred the dirt off the ladder and the house parapet from his hands to his face and his shirt, and he no longer resembled a smart wedding guest.

'I'll help you with the ladder,' he said to Mr Porlock. Perhaps he could tell his story to the innkeeper. That would not be like informing the police.

The sergeant began to eye Val suspiciously. 'I suppose you don't know anything about this?' he asked.

The direct question put Val in a fix. So he didn't reply, but just looked guilty.

'Speak up! You in with them?'

'No, sir. I've been at the wedding. My auntie's wedding at the Cock. You ask my Dad. He's in the bar. He'll tell you.'

The sergeant looked even more unbelieving. 'You don't look much like a wedding,' he said.

Val was in a real predicament. The police knew him only too well. If he admitted any knowledge now, they were sure to think he was involved in the robbery. If he said nothing, the gang would be armed and able to scarify the whole of the yard. Just like the cops to pick on me for being a boy, thought Val. Dirty old bluebottles!

But at that moment, rescue hove in sight. Taxis had been ordered to come and fetch the bridal pair and the bridesmaids, and they were now arriving at the Cock. Mum had come downstairs with the girls and Len. Auntie Glad and her husband had driven away.

'There's my Mum,' Val cried. He had never been so glad to see Mum in his life. 'You ask her.'

At the sight of police, fear leapt into Mum's eyes. 'What's he done now?' she asked.

'That's what I want to know,' said the sergeant grimly.

'I haven't done anything,' declared Val, cursing Mum for her tactless remark. 'You know I've been at the wedding all the time, Mum.'

'Some boys have broken into the shop next door,' said the sergeant. 'They've taken a rifle and a revolver out of Crabbe's shop. They got in through the roof.'

At the word 'rifle' Ally popped her head out of the taxi window, for she was already inside. 'Did you say rifle?'

'Yes. Why?'

'I bet I can guess who – '

But Mum pushed Ally back into the taxi. 'Don't you go sticking your nose into what's not your business,' she said. 'If you don't know, don't start trouble by guessing.'

Ally subsided.

'Go on, miss.' The sergeant was far politer to the pretty bridesmaid than to her brother.

'Oh, she doesn't know anything about it,' said Mum firmly, anxious to get home.

The sergeant grinned. 'All right, all right,' he said cheerfully. 'Don't you worry. We've got a good idea who it is. Had our eye on them for quite a while. We'll find out. We've got our methods.'

Mum cried, 'This taxi's ticking up,' and climbed in.

'Off you go!' said the sergeant quite paternally. 'Get the kids to bed. Where to? Magnolia Buildings? Right ahead, driver!'

Now the excitement was over, Len was half asleep and Doreen was yawning her head off.

'Never interfere when you've no call to,' Mum said to Ally.

And so ended Auntie Glad's wedding.

The next day, there was tremendous excitement in the Buildings. The police must have had their own methods after all, because they searched the homes of Shorty, Nap and

Thompson and took them all off to the police station on a charge of housebreaking and robbery.

The three boys were later sent to Borstal and approved school, according to their age, and the whole of Magnolia Buildings gave a big sigh of relief. With those three characters removed, the yard was a far happier place.

Chapter 17

JOBS

ODDLY enough, Ally and Val both got jobs in the same week. Mrs Frank down on the second balcony had the offer of a place as evening waitress in a West End café, and she suggested that Ally should baby-sit for her five evenings a week from six till eight. Ally accepted the job at once, dashing into it as she always dashed into everything, without considering any of the details.

Mrs Frank was a small, dark, Jewish woman and the baby was dark too, a pretty little girl of a year, called Rachel. She had black curls and eyes with long, dark lashes, and she took to Ally in a most flattering way. Mrs Frank was also charmed by Ally because the girl seemed so eager to please. Only the family had doubts about Ally as a baby-sitter. 'She'll sit on it and squash it flat,' said Val.

'Get on,' said Mum, 'you don't want to go shutting yourself up every evening, Al. You'd better do something with a bit more go to it.'

'But I want the cash, Mum. I've got to get some new clothes. Everybody's got new frocks. I look as old fashioned as anything. Even Lou's got one.'

Nor was Brian enthusiastic about the baby-sitting. He said, 'What d'you want to do it for, Al? It's a waste of time.'

'I've got to have some new clothes,' declared Ally, but Brian only laughed and said, 'You look all right to me.' Ally was not to be deterred. Even if Brian did go off and find another girl, she must have a new frock.

The first evening her job began, she went down in a fine state of importance to number 42, where Mrs Frank lived, and she pretended to listen to all the instructions about the baby and her food, although really she was looking round at Mrs Frank's flat and admiring her ornaments and curtains, or trying to catch a glimpse in the mirror of herself in one of Mum's overalls. Mum being much larger, the overall gave Ally a matronly look.

'Now you'll stay till Bert comes back, won't you, Ally?' finished Mrs Frank. 'He'll be back at eight. Take care of Rachel nicely, there's a good girl.' Mrs Frank kissed the baby, snatched up her muslin apron and departed.

At first Ally was quite happy. It was fun to have an empty flat all to herself. The baby was in bed and it soon went to sleep and looked a little angel, so that Ally could wander through the rooms and examine everything. She picked up the photographs and studied the faces of the Franks' friends and relations. She wandered into the Franks' bedroom and then she had a look at the kitchen. She did a bit of the mending Mrs Frank had left her, but not being very handy with her needle, she only produced terrible boggles in Mr Frank's socks.

After a while, she began to look at the clock. Only seven, one whole hour more! She read a bit from *Woman and Loveliness*, and it was still short of seven thirty. From the yard and the balconies came screams and laughter, and the sound of running feet. Everyone but Ally seemed to be having fun. She began to wonder what Brian was doing, and whether he had taken another girl to the pictures. Only by remembering her new dress, did Ally complete those two hours. She felt like the Relief of Ladysmith by the time Mr Frank came home. The baby was still asleep and he was quite pleased.

The baby was not so well behaved the second week. She was cutting teeth, and kept whimpering and would not sleep. Ally walked up and down the little room with her, up and down, up and down, singing and jigging, but Rachel still whined and grizzled. Her poor cheeks were quite scarlet, and each time she dozed off and Ally laid her carefully in the cot, she woke up at once and started to howl again. Mrs Frank was worried at having to go off and leave the child. 'But we need the money,' she said to Ally, 'and if I stay at home so soon, they may give me the sack.'

For three days Rachel wailed and was difficult until at last two neat, white pointed teeth came through. On the fourth day, when the baby might have been expected to sleep from sheer exhaustion, she was full of beans and very lively. However often Ally laid her down, she bobbed up like a celluloid doll, and started romping round her cot.

On this particular evening, Ally was deep in a very romantic story in the *Girl's Heartease Tales* series. The heroine had been rescued from every sort of peril by the hero, a most persevering young man. He had saved her from serpent-haunted caves, drug dens, lonely barges, but she had now managed to get herself suspended down a well.

At first, Ally put the baby on her knee and tried to read round and over her, but Rachel only struggled and wriggled to get to the floor. Absent-mindedly, Ally let her reach the floor, thinking it would do her no harm to crawl around a bit. It might tire her out so that she would want to sleep.

The heroine, Adrienne, was in dire straits. The rope on which the villain had hung her was fraying bit by bit. One strand went and then another. The hero meanwhile was galloping over miles of rough country, encountering robbers and flooded rivers. It did not seem that he could possibly reach the well before the last strand was severed; and Adrienne must plunge into the deep, dark waters and be drowned.

Ally read on and on. The baby was so quiet, she had forgotten about her. Yes, the hero had done it! He had found Adrienne, still hanging by a thread. 'Do not be afraid, my darling!' he cried. 'I will save you!'

The door of the flat opened and Mrs Frank came hurrying in. 'I was let off a bit early – ' she began. 'Oh my goodness!'

Ally came back to consciousness with a jerk of guilt. The baby! Out of bed and on the floor! She leapt up. And there was Rachel, black from head to foot. She had been sitting by the coal bucket contentedly licking the coal!

There was a terrible row. Ally was thrown out of the flat by Mrs Frank, who had a fine flow of language. Ally, she declared, was the idlest, wickedest, most unconscientious baby-sitter in the world. If Rachel died of coal poisoning, she would call in the police.

Still sobbing, Ally fled upstairs to Mum. It was awful! No one in the block would ever trust her again or give her another job. That hateful Rachel, what did she want to go eating coal for? And wouldn't Brian laugh when he heard! And what about the dress with only two instalments paid on it? Would the shop keep the instalments, if Ally could not finish paying for the dress?

Mum did not say I told you so. She was tactful, but later in the week, she pointed out, 'That's glamour for you. If you hadn't got reading all that trash about romance, you'd have kept your job.'

'Thought you didn't want me to have a job,' countered Ally. For by this time, the whole family thought that Ally *should* have a job, just as though the job had been their idea in the first place.

Paying the balance on the dress too was a terrible problem.

'You don't deserve a new dress,' said Mum a bit sharply when the matter came up, because she had suffered from Mrs Crawley's pointed comments. That Mrs Frank had been going round breathing fire and murder about Ally Berners, and of course, Mrs Crawley, the cat, would pass it on!

Luckily Dad, who perhaps loved Ally best of all his children, said he would give her the frock for a birthday present. So Ally dressed up in it and went off to the pictures with Brian, as proud as ten peacocks. But after this Ally did begin to see that money must be earned by good work, and that if you take on a job, it is better to do it properly.

When Val heard that Tim Robins had had the sack from his newspaper round for chronic unpunctuality, he rushed straight to the newsvendor's stall and offered himself as the new boy. This time, he did remember to wash his face and hands, and even to put on a tidy jacket. He got the job, and rose at dawn next day to go from house to house, pushing the papers through letterboxes.

When he returned home to breakfast, he was very proud of himself. He had done the round in record time. As he came into the yard, he was so cocked up with pride, that he did not bother to take the usual precautions, and so was right off his guard when Tim leapt from behind the bicycle sheds and bore him to the ground. Tim was a big, heavy, gangling type of youth.

'You dirty so-and-so!' yelled Tim. 'Going round and pinching my job. I'll learn you!' And he did with several hard punches and kicks. But Val was not so easily beaten. Once he had recovered from the shock of the attack, he fought back hard. The two of them rolled on the ground, first Tim uppermost and then Val. There was blood pouring from both their noses, and they had torn a lot more rents in their clothes.

'I'll get the police to you,' yelled old Sprot, and he started kicking at both their bodies as they revolved, hoping to stop the fight. Dad, coming downstairs on his way to work, grabbed

Val by the collar and dragged him off the ground and out of the clutches of Tim, leaving Tim still gasping and writhing on the concrete.

'He jumped out at me,' gasped Val, blood pouring from his battered face.

'He sneaked my job,' yelled Tim, scrambling up and seeming quite prepared to start the whole fight again.

'I'll learn you to keep on fighting,' growled Dad.

'I didn't start it. I don't want to fight,' said Val bitterly.

'Kicking up a flipping row in the yard,' spat out old Sprot, who was quivering with fury. 'I've never seen nothing like these young 'uns. My Dad'd have tanned the skin off me, if I'd carried on like they do. The place isn't fit for decent people to live in, I know that. It's never been the same since the war. I don't know, I'm sure.' And he shuffled off to his breakfast still muttering.

Dad now umpired the row. 'Did you get the sack or not?' he asked Tim in his slow voice.

'Well.' Tim wriggled and mopped his nose with his sleeve. 'Mr Arby did say . . .'

'Did you get the sack or not?'

'If Val hadn't come butting in, Mr Arby'd have had me back.'

'So you did get the sack. Well, I don't see you've got anything to complain of. You leave my Val alone in future or I'll speak to your Dad. Got that?'

Tim seemed to have got it, for he went off quickly and didn't look back.

'It was bad enough when you weren't working,' said Dad surveying his blood-stained son dispassionately. 'But it's worse now you are. Cor, you and Ally! I don't know what's going to happen to you.'

Chapter 18

THE BONFIRE

OF course, there was only one thought in all the children's minds as November approached – Guy Fawkes Day!

Most of the boys made up bundles with masks and old hats, and borrowing prams, went round pushing their Guys. Once the boys had staked out a claim to a certain good corner, such as by the cinema, or along under the Cock, they fought tooth and nail to preserve their pitch. Every few yards during the end of October, there would be children sitting with monstrous looking dummies, crying 'Penny for the Guy, sir! Penny for the Guy!' The nastier children shouted rude remarks after people who refused their begging.

In one way or another, enormous sums of money were collected. Then the children rushed round to the firework shop and laid in huge supplies of rockets and wheels and fizzers and bangers and hoppers. Of course, not everyone could wait until the Fifth and most evenings for quite three weeks, boys were letting off odd fireworks just to see if they really did explode.

The radio announcers were already giving out instructions to people about not inventing their own fireworks, as these would be dangerous. And the fire brigades were making preparations because they knew the Fifth would be a real field day.

Of course, Val and his gang were very busy over their collecting. They were especially looking forward to the Fifth this year as there would be no Shorty's gang to sabotage them. Val and George had concocted such a horrible looking guy that people paled at the sight of it, and paid up quickly so they might hurry on and not have to look at it. George had borrowed the old family pram, and the boys trundled their guy every day from four o'clock to bedtime. They were not just static beggars, either, who sat merely guarding their guy and cap of pennies. They were highly mobile and rushed up to passers by, importuning them so fiercely that they got nervous and forked out sixpences and shillings by mistake, and then went home and wrote angry letters to the papers saying that Guy Fawkes Day was a scandal and was teaching the younger generation to beg.

But fireworks were not the only thing that Val had in mind for the Fifth. He was also planning a mammoth bonfire, and bonfires were of course absolutely forbidden. Luckily there happened to be a large bomb site down beyond Magnolia Buildings. It had been cleared so as to be ready for some new Council flats. It was here that Val meant to have his fire, but it must be carefully organized so that the police or the fire brigade did not stop it.

One of the problems of living in a large town is how to get rid of large scale rubbish. The dustmen exact big tips for taking away worm-eaten sofas and chairs. Val knew this, and for some time he had been canvassing all the flats for junk. A week before the Fifth, he had got his gang to manhandle the old furniture downstairs and into the bicycle shed. Nobody asked where the rubbish was going. They did not want to, being only too pleased to avoid tipping the dustmen. Soon the bicycle shed was stuffed to overflowing. The boys were to muster the last of the junk on the evening of the Fifth itself.

There were about twenty school age boys in the Buildings and Val, who was a natural organizer, collected them together.

'You're to be in the yard as soon as it's getting dark,' he ordered. 'And if you start blabbing about our plans, Billy – well, you know what! So keep all your big mouths shut, see! No, you can't, Ginger, you're too small. You and Reg can scout ahead and see if the coast's clear and no cops about. The rest of us'll take the stuff along.'

At nightfall on the Fifth, when the sky was already full of falling stars and loud bangs, a very strange procession could have been seen leaving Magnolia Buildings. Old sofas, chairs, beds, whatnots, mattresses were all moving down the street above short, trotting legs. Val and George led with a horrible sofa that was burst and bulging hair and flock. Four smaller boys lugged a huge mattress. Billy had two old chairs, while Ginger frisked about ahead giving imaginary warnings.

The official order was that the procession should proceed in silence, but this was quite impossible for twenty boys. There were giggles, crashes, and collisions, as the furniture bumped itself into the railings or into other moving pieces.

'Cor, shut up, you asses! Come on, hurry!' adjured Val. 'I'll bash you, Bill. You take my end of the sofa, Pete, I'm going ahead.'

A fight had started between two boys carrying chairs, but it soon stopped as the procession moved steadily over the combatants. Fortunately all the grown-ups were indoors having their tea, so the procession got safely to the bomb site.

'Come on, chaps, pile it up,' hissed Val, as they staggered into the centre of the site. 'No! Not like that. Here, stick the

big stuff underneath, and the small stuff on top. Buck up, or they'll come and stop us. Stop mucking about and get on with it.'

All the chairs and sofas were somehow erected into a pyre,

and the hideous Guy that had done such a good begging job was hoisted to the very top and posed there on a chair with three legs. A rocket was stuck in the Guy's arms and a sparkler on his head. From somewhere Val conjured up a tin of paraffin, and he struck the first match, while the others shoved and grabbed trying to get at the match box.

At one moment, the bomb site had been a dark, bare area with a few shadowy figures lugging heavy objects, and then – as the match tickled up the paraffin, fire leapt out. In a moment the whole place was a wild inferno of crackling flames, jumping squibs, shooting rockets, bouncing bangers, and whizzers. Dozens of demonic figures yelled and ran and leapt about, for in a few seconds the children had multiplied into hundreds.

Up, up, shot the flames, sending great sprays and showers of sparks into the night. All the old chairs, full of worm, beetle, and dry horse hair, caught like tinder and made a glowing core to the fire. Whizzers and bangers were now going off all over the place, exploding like jumping jacks in the very middle of the crowd, and starting yells of dismay and small fights. Screaming girls ran away and were pursued. All the windows in the houses around the bomb site had shot up, and their inhabitants were yelling protests and complaints, but not one of the children listened. Some of the adults saw the fun of the fire, but the duller ones, who were only greedy for their rights as citizens, rang up the police, the fire brigade, the Vicar or anyone else they fancied.

Val and his gang were in their glory. For weeks they had been planning this night, counting their pennies and dreaming of rockets. Their faces and hands were by now, if possible, blacker than usual. As the rockets went up and broke into a myriad of coloured stars, red, green, and orange, their hearts seemed to soar too and explode in sparks of pleasure.

Yet hardly had the fire attained its full height, before the children heard the ringing of the engines' bells. Huge, red machines were rushing from every direction towards the bomb site.

'They're coming!' yelled Val. 'Look out, chaps, the brigade's here.' Close behind the brigade were the black police cars.

Usually the boys would have run away. Mum, who had come down with Len, held her breath, certain the boys would be in more trouble. But the boys did not care. They knew that public opinion and history and tradition were all on their side. Besides, on this night they were seized with such excitement that they felt a week in the cells was worth such a conflagration as they had raised.

All the officials had leapt out of their vehicles, the firemen prepared to drag the long hoses towards the flames. From the windows above the chorus of yelled abuse and denunciation grew louder.

But for a few moments the men in uniform stayed their hands. They were remembering their own childhood, when they too had searched vainly for somewhere to light a great fire.

'They aren't after doing much harm then,' said Paddy, one of the brigade. 'They're away from the houses, so they are.'

'This is Council property,' said one of the police. 'They are trespassing. They ought not to be here.' But really there were too many children to arrest.

'Poor kids,' said the sergeant, who was also a father. 'They've been saving their pennies and begging for weeks.'

'They oughtn't to be let go begging,' said the first policeman, who had strong views on vagrancy.

Some of the more angry of the neighbours, who were annoyed that the fire still burned, had come out of the houses and were shouting at the police.

'They're dirtying our windows. They're smutting our washing. They've woken our babies and frightened our dogs. They ought to be punished. My father'd have leathered 'em! It's dangerous. It's a waste of money – a disgrace. I am a ratepayer. I shall write to my M.P.' And so on and so on.

At last, the police and the fire brigade moved slowly in, but they still seemed reluctant to quench the flames. It was as

though they too were hypnotized by the fire. The children had fallen quiet, and were no longer leaping and yelling because they were a little afraid. The sergeant had shouted, 'You know you can't light a fire here.' But the children knew they had. Then the fire began to die down of itself, because it had burnt so fiercely. The highest chair toppled and the guy astride of it let off his rocket, tilted, fell and was consumed in the fire's core. As the guy fell, it seemed to be a signal for the men to quench the flames. But no one minded so much now. The boys had had their fire and let off most of their rockets. They were fairly willing to go in to bed. Guy Fawkes had been burnt until another year.

Chapter 19

THE PANTOMIME

THE shops always felt it was Christmas time long before anyone else. Some people laughed and said that the shops were silly, that Christmas was getting earlier and earlier, and soon it would begin in August. But the children agreed with the shops, because they too liked to think about the coming of Christmas. It was the one bright star ahead that kept them cheerful through dark, smoggy November and icy December.

The Common was almost deserted now except for a few people taking short cuts across to their work. A few blue-nosed, blue-kneed footballers might run about there, but the sailing boats and the dominoes were put away. Even the prams preferred to go for walks along the lighted shops. Most of the fallen leaves had been swept up, the little cafés had shut, and the bandstand was deserted. No children were swinging on the swings or sliding down the slides, no lovers were wandering in the thickets, because for some days the darkness of Egypt had closed in. No wonder that people turned to indoor occupations, TV, dancing, whist, roller skating, cinemas and pin tables.

The Berners family were used to London winters and smog, and did not worry very much. They were too busy. Mum had gone back to her cleaning, and although she might groan a bit when she turned out into the icy darkness of five a.m., as soon as she was in the lighted bus with the other cleaners, all off to their snug, centrally-heated offices, she was gay again and full of backchat. 'Didn't half miss you, ducks,' said the fat conductor.

Val was getting up early too, doing his paper round. He never failed to be there and Mr Arby said he was a good boy. Sometimes, he longed to stay in bed and not to go out into the smog or frost or rain, but the thought of twelve shillings a week spurred him on. He was saving up to buy a tent so that next summer he could go camping in the country. With a tent and a bike he would have the freedom of the whole world. The faithful George would go with him. Already they had made a plan to join the navy together as soon as they could.

Mum had claimed part of Val's money to pay for his new shoes. 'It's not fair,' he grumbled. 'I'm not working for shoes.'

'Then you can go barefoot,' said Mum, laughing. 'Suppose I kept my money for myself?'

Doreen had to rise early too, because she had a long journey to the Green Coats School, and even when she came back late in the evening, she still had a great deal of homework, so that her eyes grew pink at the edges from over-reading.

Len was quite happy because Mum had promised to buy him a budgerigar for Christmas, as that was the only sort of pet that Mr Sprot allowed in the flats. 'I'll teach him to talk,' said Len, gloating over the thought of his new pet.

'Let's hope when Len's got his budgie,' said Mum, 'that he'll stop bringing things home. I mean what with black kids and stray dogs, this place is the Lost Property Office.'

Nobody asked Dad if he were happy. Maybe he did not know if he were or not. But he was probably quite content as long as he could be with his family, and go along to his usual corner at the Cock in the evenings.

Auntie Glad seemed very happy indeed. When she and Uncle William came over to tea on a Sunday, they were full of the wall-papering and painting that was going on in the villa. Uncle William looked fatter and more beaming than ever and Auntie Glad had never gone back to wearing her black crochet cap. Aggie had now made it up with her brother.

'Though I wish she hadn't,' said Auntie Glad naughtily to Mum. 'Because she's always round our place telling me how to make Bill comfortable, as if I don't know. Still, there's a bone in every marriage, and if Bill wants to see her, he's welcome.'

But what about Ally? Was she happy too? Not all the

time unfortunately. Take, for instance, the school pantomime.

The school had always done a nativity play every Christmas, and for two years Ally had been the Virgin. This year it had been decided to do a pantomime, and Ally was sure she would be chosen to play the principal girl.

'Look, I'm very sorry, Gloria,' Miss Fleetwood had said when they were casting. 'But you really are too tall. Linda is the only one with the voice and the legs for principal boy, and you're half a head taller than she is. I don't think we can make you an Ugly Sister, because the boys will do them. So that leaves the Good Fairy.'

Ally's eyes filled with tears. 'Oh, Miss Fleetwood, you almost promised me I'd be Cinderella. I don't want to be the Good Fairy, that's a soppy part.'

'But, Ally,' said Miss Fleetwood, 'I couldn't help your sprouting up so fast, could I? Come on now, be a good girl and make the best of it. I'll get Mr Browne to write you in a nice, long piece as Fairy Godmother. Anyhow, you'll have a lovely dress, all tinsel silver and white and a crown on your head. I think we can fix you a wand with an electric battery so the star at the top lights up. You'll be able to do a dance and you'll get a special spotlight every time you come on.'

Ally blinked back her tears. It wasn't fair! Not even a special spotlight would make up for being Fairy Godmother. She had always wanted to play Cinderella, and had imagined herself in a beautiful gown at the Court Ball, with the parents thinking how lovely Ally Berners was! That would have been true glamour. In this panto, the Fairy spent a lot of her time dressed up as an ugly old witch. She was not transformed into a real fairy until late in the second act.

Ally went to Brian about her disappointment, but he could not take it seriously. 'It's only a kid's play at school,' he said, with the grandeur of someone who is just leaving the Grammar School and perhaps going to London University.

'You don't understand,' said Ally, as they were walking back from the pictures. 'Suppose a talent scout should just happen to be in the audience. You never know. I was reading the other day about Glamorna Earle who was spotted while being a waitress. And if I did a really good Cinderella, I might be taken off to Hollywood and become a star.'

'Nonsense!' cried Brian derisively. 'Can you see any talent scout going to the Church School panto? Be your age, Al.'

But Ally persisted. 'He might be a parent, you never know. I ought to get a chance. None of the other girls can act for toffee.'

Even if the school did not contain many good actors, it was thinking and talking of nothing else but the panto. The boys in the carpentry class were making the scenery and the art classes were painting it. Even the needlework classes were running up tinselled toutous instead of the usual overalls and shoe bags. Rehearsals filled every spare moment. Luckily, Mr Browne, the headmaster and producer, was a very talented man and knew quite a lot about directing. During the last two years he had managed to raise a school orchestra and taught it to play a few tunes. Miss Fleetwood was good on clothes, and with the help of some of the other teachers had fashioned wonderful costumes from odds and ends.

'We've got a huge theatrical wardrobe at home, and I can borrow from that,' she explained. 'You see, a parish always needs money, so we used to do a lot of acting.'

In spite of having the wrong part, Ally went round the flat singing the song refrains at the top of her voice, until Mum yelled, 'For pity's sake lay off, Ally. I'm sick to death of those choruses.'

'And it isn't fair,' said Ally for the thousandth time. 'You know that Ann Price who's playing Cinderella? She hasn't a clue, the silly little thing. I could act her off the stage. They'll be sorry they didn't have me.'

'They ought to have put on Jack and the Beanstalk,' said Val. 'Then you could've been the beanstalk, Al.'

There were all the usual excitements and horrors of putting on a panto: some people did not learn their words, the scenery went smudgy, the principal characters got flu, the flood lights did not arrive, the tickets were late back from the printers. All these disasters happened. The dress rehearsal was of course, simply awful, just as dress rehearsals always are. The lights fused because there was too big a load, some of the costumes were still not finished, and the Principal Boy kept fluffing his lines. The Ugly Sisters who had been so funny at the first rehearsals were getting duller and duller. In fact, everything seemed hopeless. Mr Browne and Miss Fleetwood went round saying, 'It will be all right on the night,' but they did not sound as if they believed it.

All the classrooms were turned into dressing rooms, and suddenly their chalky, sooty smell was overlaid by scents of grease paint and powder. It was quite amazing to see untidy, grubby school-children turning into entrancing fairies, or Court ladies with dazzling complexions. Each child as it was made up went to the mirror to see the transformation with a joyful unbelief. At last the make believe of the play seemed true. But under the beautiful, dressed-up exteriors were frightened, thumping hearts. Everyone was wondering, suppose I make a mess of my part, suppose I forget my words?

Ally certainly looked dazzling in her silver and white, with all her golden hair arranged beneath a shining coronet; but her magnificence had to be masked by a great black cloak, a false nose and witch's hat.

All her old self pity came back when she looked across at Cinderella. How could silly little Ann put it over? There she was, as smug as a pug, with her stupid doll-face prettiness.

Ally had to go and take her place above the mock chimney-piece. She had to come down the chimney and to appear on the hearth with a loud explosion and a flash. While she waited, poised ready to jump, she could hear the exciting murmur of a packed house. In every chair was a parent who had come to wait for the entrance of their own child. I ought to be playing Cinderella, Ally kept thinking, and a lump of anger came into her throat.

The excited buzz of talk was drowned by the school orchestra that scratched its way carefully through a minuet. If all the instruments did not finish the tune at absolutely the same second, who cared? It was so miraculous that the school should have an orchestra at all. The curtain suddenly went up, and a

wave of hot air from the crowded audience blew across the cool stage. Now the Ugly Sisters went on, prancing about in their comic petticoats and frilled pants, while poor little Cinderella was trying to dress them for the ball.

Even from behind her chimney, Ally knew that the panto was going well. Something had happened to everyone, excitement had gone to their heads, and was making them act and sing and dance as they had never done before. The jokes were going over and the audience was laughing nicely. Listening to all this, Ally turned from a Good to a Bad Fairy. She ought to be out there singing Cinderella's song instead of crouching up the chimney.

Now the Ugly Sisters were dressed at last, in spite of all the queer things that had happened to their clothes while they were trying to get into them. They were tap dancing off to the ball, followed by the Wicked Stepmother and the Buttons. Cinderella was left in her rags, to sing her plaintive song in the ashes.

'I cannot go to the Ball.
Sisters and Mamma and all
Will polka and lancer,
And have lots of fun.
I shall sit here
And just eat a dry bun.
I shall not dance with a handsome young feller
But stay in the ashes and be Cinderella.
Oh, I do want to go to the Ball!'

This was the Good Fairy's cue. Ally gathered herself up, broomstick and all. When the big flash and explosion came, she was down the chimney and standing on the hearth in her spotlight. To the dazzled audience this appearance seemed a miracle.

Whatever it was that had got into the rest of the actors, had got into Ally too, only more so. Ally was a natural actress. Her vivid imagination was not cramped by any shyness.

In her disappointment, she had rather slouched through rehearsals, only doing the minimum of work, but tonight the devil of jealousy was in her. She was quite possessed. She would show them. She would act that silly little Cinderella off the stage.

Ally just gave that Fairy Godmother all she had. If the panto had been going quite well before, it now went with a bang! She burlesqued it, she over-acted it, she caricatured all the Good Fairies there had ever been, she played the fool, she made the audience die of laughing because she just did not care. And because she did not care, she could do anything she liked with them.

This was very naughty of Ally, because from the moment she stepped on to the stage, she gave that panto a twist that pulled it all out of shape. From the laughing, roaring audience, Ally drew fresh ideas, thought of all sorts of gags that she had never done before. Poor little Cinderella was so bewildered that she could hardly get out her lines, and anyhow the audience was laughing so much at Ally's improvisations that they could not concentrate on Cinderella at all.

It was no good Miss Fleetwood catching Ally between scenes and imploring her to behave, no good for Mr Browne to tick her off, for that night she had gone mad and did not care. It serves them all right, she said to herself, they should have given me a proper part and this wouldn't have happened. Besides, the audience was adoring her. They were just lapping it up. All the parents who had come along from a sense of duty were enjoying themselves as much as if they were at Drury Lane.

Ally went up and sang her song that was full of good wishes for Cinderella so satirically that it could have been taken for a series of curses. When she sang that she hoped the girl would get her prince, the audience knew that the prince was a milk-sop anyway and no good to any girl. Ally's goings on had so gingered up the Ugly Sisters that they were also getting above themselves.

When Mr Browne played a tune on the piano in the interval, he thumped into it all the fury he felt against Ally Berners. But there was no stopping her because she certainly had the audience on her side. The headmaster could hear the audience asking each other, 'Who is the Fairy Godmother? Isn't she a scream?'

In the interval, Cinderella and the Prince attacked Ally. 'What do you think you're doing?' they cried. 'You never give us our proper cues or anything, and stop playing up those silly tricks, riding round the stage on your broomstick. You've never done that before. We didn't know when to come in.'

But Ally paid no attention and just went on to the stage with a mocking laugh.

During the second part of the panto, she was just as outrageous as ever. She pranced her way through the Court Ball, and upset the Court ladies so that they forgot their dance. By the time the show came to an end, and Ally had to speak her epilogue in front of the curtain, the audience was practically standing up and yelling for her. Never had there been such a school panto! Behind the scenes, Mr Browne and Miss Fleet-

wood were biting their nails and wishing they could take a stick to her.

Mum and Len were quite overwhelmed by the brilliance of Ally, and nearly clapped their hands off. They, like the rest of the audience, had no idea how she had disrupted the cast. The actors themselves were waiting with claws out in the dressing rooms, and there would have been a free fight if the children had not been suppressed by the teachers.

'Ally, come into my study a minute,' said Mr Browne. 'You have gone a bit too far.'

'I don't care,' said Ally with brilliant eyes and the freedom of a pupil who has only one more day of school life. 'I ought to have had the lead. Anyhow, I made the show. You can't say I didn't, sir. Listen to them now.' This was undoubtedly true, because the audience was still clapping and shouting for the Fairy Godmother. 'I think perhaps I should go out and take another curtain, sir?' And she pranced off.

'If you don't promise to behave properly tomorrow night, I'll put in an understudy,' cried Mr Browne.

'You can't,' said naughty Ally, quite drunk with success. 'They'll all come to see me.'

Ally was very wild and elated all the way home, even though Lou was worried and told her, 'You won't half cop it tomorrow, Al.'

'Why should I?' Ally hopped along the road. 'I showed them I could act.'

'Mr Browne'll give you a bad leaving report,' said Lou, 'and that may muck up you getting a good job.'

'Pooh!' cried Ally, because she knew that she would be going on the stage. The great West End producers would not care about a schoolmaster's report.

Chapter 20

FAME AND AFTERWARDS

ODDLY enough, there had been by chance a reporter in the audience, one of the reporters of the South London press who had a small girl at the school. He had gone off to the panto with the utmost unwillingness because his daughter was a fairy. He guessed at the boredom of listening for two hours while children stumbled over half-forgotten lines. As it was he had been completely captivated by the bewitching Ally.

'She's a new Beatrice Lillie, a Nellie Wallace in the embryo,' he said excitedly to his wife on the way home. 'It's quite amazing! That girl is a real find. She's got vitality, imagination and fun in her as well as a warmth of personality that comes straight across to the audience. That warmth is very rare. Few people have it. That's a girl who should go on the stage. I'd like some manager to see her. She's darned pretty too. I've never seen such hair.' And he sat down late that night and wrote such an amusing paragraph about the school panto and Ally that it was printed by most of the South London papers. Everyone round the Common read that Ally was a brilliant young actress.

Mum was hardly back from work next day, when Mrs Doherty and other neighbours came running in with their papers.

'Cor,' said Mum when she read the paragraph. 'Fancy them writing all that about our Ally!'

'He says it's the West End theatres she should be in,' cried Mrs Doherty. 'Or the TV now. There's lovely she'd be on TV and us watching her that knew her from the cradle. That'd be a pride for ye, Mrs Berners, dear.'

Ally, who when she calmed down, had begun to feel slightly guilty, was now almost delirious with delight. So, after all, she was justified. According to the reporter, she had made the pantomime, and how could the school staff and the children disapprove of that? The show was certain to be packed tonight. Mr Browne might even run it for an extra evening. Ally's wild and vivid imagination was off at full gallop. She saw other people, important people, reading the paper, theatrical managers arriving in Rolls Royces to offer her engagements at huge salaries. She was wearing a mink coat and just leaving for Hollywood by plane. 'Miss Gloria Berners when asked her plans, said, "I really do not know at present what I shall decide to do. I feel that perhaps I should not refuse Filmland's offer." '

But not everyone was impressed by the newspapers. Some of the children had gone home in a rage and reported the whole case against Ally. The parents of the slighted actors were very sour. Cinderella's father even had a word with Ally's Dad when they met in the yard. 'Your girl properly mucked up things for my Ann last night.'

'Did you see the papers this morning?' asked Dad triumphantly. 'They said our Glory made the show.'

'She may of,' cried the other father furiously. 'But at other people's expense, if you ask me.'

'Well, I don't ask you,' said Dad, which finished that conversation.

There were no ordinary lessons on the day of the pantomime's second showing, and Ally took good care not to go to the dressing room too soon. She was a bit afraid of her reception there. Actually, the children were not as hostile as she had feared. They too had read the papers, and had been impressed by them. If the papers said Ally was so good, then she must be.

Mr Browne and Miss Fleetwood were still very chilly and cross, but they dared not make a big fuss, because they did not want to upset the nerves of the cast just before the show. Ally could be ticked off afterwards. Anyhow she had made a big hit and there was sure to be a large attendance on this second evening. The tickets had sold like hot cakes.

When Ally went to her position above the big chimney, she was in a mixed frame of mind. If the other children had been horrid to her, she would have found it easier to defy everyone. She still wanted to do her best and to be the star part, but she did not want to antagonize her friends permanently. She had always been popular and she did not care to lose that popularity. Also the first mad excitement and resentment had died out of her. She was in two minds as to how she should play her part that night.

As a result, the whole of the show went wrong. The rest of the cast was now waiting and ready for Ally's tricks and nonsense, and were prepared to stand by and pick up such cues as she should deign to throw them. Ally herself tried to be wild and funny and to keep up the burlesque, but what had been created by resentment she could not reproduce in cold blood. It takes a professional to reproduce the same emotions night after night. Ally had lost her self assurance with her anger, and the uncertainty in her went straight across to her audience who somehow felt uncomfortable and did not laugh as they had the night before. Most of them had come expecting something wonderful, and having set their hopes so high, were soon disappointed, and their disappointment was mirrored back to the actors, who became flatter still.

In the second act, Ally tried again to do her wild witch's ride round the stage, but this time she was clumsy, somehow tripped over the broomstick, and fell heavily, her right arm twisted awkwardly beneath her and catching her whole weight. She could not help it, but she gave a loud shriek of pain.

A searing agony shot through her shoulder. She tried to roll over and free herself but found she could not, and screamed. The audience burst into a babble, and Miss Fleetwood rang down the curtain. Ally was carried into the headmaster's study. In two different ways on both days, she had managed to wreck the show.

Ally was crying with pain while the audience was dispersing and the children getting out of their clothes in the classroom. 'Oh, it hurts, it hurts,' she sobbed, for the agony on top of the nervous strain was too much for her.

'I think she must have dislocated her shoulder. A dislocation is often far more painful than a break,' said Mr Browne, looking very worried. 'I'll ring for the ambulance, and we'd better get her across to the hospital and have her arm X-rayed at once. Miss Fleetwood, send someone across to fetch her mother.'

The ambulance arrived before Mum, because she had had to settle the family first and change her clothes. The men lifted Ally, who was still wearing her fairy dress, gently into the ambulance; but there was no position in which she was comfortable. At the hospital, she was carried first to the X-ray department, where they discovered it was a bad dislocation, and then taken to the theatre. A prick in the arm put her to sleep, and when she woke up again, she was in bed in the Women's Ward, and her dislocation had been reduced. But oh, how it did ache!

She was allowed to go home in a couple of days, and her arm soon mended, but she had to spend most of her Christmas holidays having massage.

'Well,' said Mum, after Christmas, when Ally's arm was out of plaster. 'Doesn't look as though Hollywood's going to make you an offer. I'm going over to see if they'll take you at Louise's. I heard they were wanting an apprentice there in the ladies' hairdressing saloon. So if it's glamour you want, my girl, you'd get it. Just suit you, I reckon, and you'd see a bit of life into the bargain. But don't you come home with your hair dyed sky pink or some such nonsense, or Dad'll tan the hide off you. And don't get up to none of your contraptions neither.'

Ally dared not say that she wanted to go on the stage. Her pride having had such a fall, she was frightened of being laughed at. True, a dislocated shoulder had been exciting if very painful, and Mr Browne, considering the girl had been punished enough, had spared her in his report. All he had stated about Gloria Berners was that she had a tendency to over-enthusiasm.

To work in Louise's was not as exciting as Hollywood, but a great deal better than many other jobs, so Ally went off to her apprenticeship with quite a light heart. She had always liked fiddling about with her hair, and possessing such golden curls had encouraged her interest.

A few weeks at Louise's altered her a great deal. She now went about looking neat and elegant, with properly manicured finger nails and expertly cut hair. She also collected so much gossip from the customers that Mum was kept well entertained.

'Do you know what?' Ally came bursting into the flat one evening in March. 'I saw Mr Collins today, he's the manager, you know, and he says if I go on as I'm going, he'll get me into the West End branch. It's my hair. He thinks it will encourage the customers. Oh, Mum! The West End!'

'There,' cried Mum, looking with delight at her pretty daughter. 'I believe you kids are going to turn out all right after all. What with Doreen being a school teacher, and Val going for a sailor, and you getting to the West End. Why, Ally, you may meet a Duke or someone grand, and get married and be a posh lady!'

'What, me!' cried Ally in mock scorn. But her eyes were dancing and she looked as though she half believed her mother's words.

ABOUT THE AUTHOR

Elizabeth Stucley comes from North Devon, where her family have lived for centuries, and she has Norman knights, Elizabethan pirates, and Sir Richard Grenville of the *Revenge* among her ancestors.

She has had a very varied career. She has nursed a constituency for the Conservative Party, run the local Girl Guides for fourteen years, taught in schools, done a lot of escaping during the war when she was a driver for the French army, cooked for the British army, done occupational therapy with children, and written several books.

She now lives in Bath, but she used to live in a lovely house on Clapham Common designed by Sir Christopher Wren. While she lived there she used to keep open house for the children who lived near her in Clapham, and she wrote this book for them and about them. They formed The Adventurers' Club, and acted plays, painted, and went camping and on many expeditions.

PSSST